THE BODY
Wellness

HOLISTIC APPROACHES TO ACHIEVING
OPTIMAL HEALTH AND VITALITY

WILLIE SEALS

Copyright © 2024 Willie Seals.

All rights reserved. No part of this book may be reproduced, stored, or transmitted by any means—whether auditory, graphic, mechanical, or electronic—without written permission of both publisher and author, except in the case of brief excerpts used in critical articles and reviews. Unauthorized reproduction of any part of this work is illegal and is punishable by law.

ISBN: 979-8-89419-382-3 (sc)
ISBN: 979-8-89419-383-0 (hc)
ISBN: 979-8-89419-384-7 (e)

Because of the dynamic nature of the Internet, any web addresses or links contained in this book may have changed since publication and may no longer be valid. The views expressed in this work are solely those of the author and do not necessarily reflect the views of the publisher, and the publisher hereby disclaims any responsibility for them.

One Galleria Blvd., Suite 1900, Metairie, LA 70001
(504) 702-6708

CONTENTS

Acid Reflux 1
Aging 2
Angiogram 3
Arugula 4
Asthma 5
Asthma 2 6
Astigmatism 7
Back Pain 8
Bananas 9
Benefits of Eating Strawberries 10
Benefits of Turmeric 11
Birth 12
Body Building Strength 13
Body Fat 14
Blood Clots 15
Blood Sugar 16
Blood Work 17
Burning Fat 18
Canned Foods 19
Chiropractor 20
Congenital Insensitivity to Pain 21
Congestion 22
Constipation 23
Cortisone 24
Cortisone Injections 25
Cough 26
Dealing with Pain 27
Dehydration 28
Diabetes 29
DKA 30
Do the Best You Can! 31
Eating 32
Effects of Alcohol 33

Exercise	34
Fake Food	35
Fasting Goals	36
Feeling Good	37
Fighting Fair	38
Flu	39
Fresh Air	40
Fuel Your Vessel	41
Going to the Doctor	42
Gut Health!	43
Headaches	44
Health Program	45
Healthy Living	46
Healthy Mouth	47
Heartburn	48
Heart	49
Heavy Metals	50
Herbs	51
Hereditary	52
Holistic Practice	53
Home Remedy on How to Get Rid of Phlegm	54
Hunger	55
Inflammation	57
Kidney Stones	58
Knee Pain	59
Lemon Water	60
Living Water	61
Living with Diabetes	62
Losing Weight	63
Meditation	64
Menopause	65
Mental Health	66
Migraine	67
Moderation	68
Moderation 2	69
More Energy	70
Mosquito Bites	71

Nightcaps	72
Nosebleed	73
Number 2	74
Nutrition	75
Obesity	76
Osteoarthritis	77
Our Belly!	78
Oxygen	79
Pain	80
Parasite	81
Periodontist	82
Plantar Fasciitis	83
Pneumonia	84
Push Through The Pain	85
Push Yourself	86
Reflexology	87
REM Sleep	88
RNA	89
Root Canal	90
Sadness	91
Salt Body	92
Sea Moss	93
Shower	94
Sickle Cell Anemia	95
Sleep Apnea	96
Sleep	97
Slow Down	98
Snake Venom	99
Sore Throat	100
Spirit of Laziness	101
Spring Cleaning The Body	102
Stiffness	103
Stingray Stings	104
Stomach Pain	105
Stomach Virus	106
Stress	107
Stroke	108

Salt, Sugar, And Stress 109
Suicide...110
The Sun...112
Swimming 113
Taking Care of Yourself...114
Testosterone 115
Third Eye 116
Therapist...117
Tired 118
Tune-Up..119
Viruses 120
Walking 121
Water 122
Why is Aluminum in Products? 123
Work it Out 124
Workout..125
Work Through It 126
You Need Rest...127
Zinc 128

Body

HEALTH/WELLNESS

ACID REFLUX

....

Acid reflux is heartburn caused by a backflow, or reflux, of stomach acid into your esophagus. Symptoms include burning pain in your chest that usually occurs after eating and worsens when lying down. Acid reflux is caused by weakness or relaxation of your lower esophagus. Normally, this valve closes tightly after food enters your stomach. If it relaxes when it shouldn't, your stomach contents rise back up into your esophagus, which causes you to throw up and feel miserable. A balanced diet with vegetables and protein is best for acid reflux. Veggies such as lettuce, celery, and sweet peppers are easy on the stomach and won't cause painful gas. Drink caffeine-free ginger tea or chew on low-sugar dry ginger for a natural tummy tamer. Try to stay away from fried foods like onion rings and fries. Avoid eating anything two hours before you go to bed. If the problem persists, please see your physician. If you are working on something you really care about, you don't have to be pushed. The vision pushes you.

Head Shepherd
P.O.G.
Loving Ministry

Body

HEALTH/WELLNESS

AGING

....

It's believed religion is the reason people give up on life. It's the agony of being lonely. In the 2009 medical journal, aging is categorized as a disease. They said dying by aging is caused by disease and the food we eat. We all know the obvious signs of aging: wrinkles, gray hair, a slightly stooped posture, perhaps some senior moments of forgetfulness. You can enjoy a better body by knowing what's natural as you age and what's not and by learning simple steps to combat aging. You can try to delay or lessen the changes by staying active. Walking, running, swimming, or even a little moderate exercise each day can help you stay at a good weight and keep your blood pressure down. Eat lots of fruits, vegetables, and whole grains to keep your heart healthy. Some herbs that can help you with aging include astragalus and jiaogulan. Astragalus is an anti-inflammatory Chinese medicine for the joints that also boosts the immune system. It can help treat many other different illnesses as well. Jiaogulan is an herbal tea. Scientific studies prove the amazing health benefits of jiaogulan, including improved circulation, better sleep, a supercharged immune system, healthy blood pressure, and overall enhanced longevity. Stop aging by not worrying about life, and put it in God's hands. Live your best life now!

Head Shepherd
P.O.G.
Loving Ministry

Body

HEALTH/WELLNESS

ANGIOGRAM

....

An angiogram is a procedure that uses X-ray images to look for blockages in your blood vessels. Your health care provider may want to do an angiogram when you have signs of blocked or abnormal areteries or veins. Angiograms help providers determine the source of the problem and the extent of the damage to your blood vessels. This can lead to the diagnosis of issues such as coronary artery disease, atherosclerosis, blood clots, or an aneurysm. The procedure is usually performed by an interventional cardiologist. An angiogram involves injecting contrast dye that your provider can see with an X-ray machine. That is how the doctor can see if you have a blockage in your blood vessels. The procedure is done with a catheter, a long slender tube that will go through your groin and slide into a large artery. If you know anyone who has a history of heart disease or is having chest pains frequently, please tell them to go see your local cardiologist. You are the master of your own destiny. Use your strength well. They are the keys to your destiny and your success in life. Your heart drives your body, so take care of it!

Head Shepherd
P.O.G.
Loving Ministry

Body

HEALTH/WELLNESS

ARUGULA

Nothing is impossible. The word itself says, "I am possible." Arugula, a type of plant that has too many leaves, belongs to the family Brassicaceae. It is closely related to cauliflower, kale, and radishes. Depending on where you are in the world, you may know this leafy vegetable, but with a different name. Other names for arugula include colewort, roquette and rocket. Arugula may seem like a fancier type of lettuce, but keep in mind that not all greens are lettuce. Many people choose to consume this cruciferous vegetable frequently, as it provides a lot of health benefits. Arugula is an excellent source of antioxidants, which is why it's a great detoxifier. It also contains nutritients that may reduce cancer risk, boost heart health, help prevent osteoporosis, reduce the risk of diabetes, and improve athletic performance. There's no miracle. When it comes to weight loss, eating more fruits and vegetables like arugula can help. The green veggie is low in calories. The bottom line: the benefits of eating more greens like arugula far outweigh the risk. You will never exceed the person you decided to be.

Head Shepherd
P.O.G.
Loving Ministry

Body

HEALTH/WELLNESS

ASTHMA

....

To all the dreamers out there: don't ever let the world's negativity disenchant you or your spirit. If you surround yourself with love and the right people, anything is possible. When your chest feels tight and it's difficult to breathe, it may be a sign that airway inflammation is present. While an asthma attack may be triggered by many things, airway inflammation is frequently a cause. Asthma affects people of all ages; although it often starts in childhood, it can also develop for the first time in adults. There's currently no cure, but there are simple treatments that can help keep the symptoms under control so it does not have an overwhelming impact on your life. Many people use Earth plants, herbs, and natural dietary supplements, especially Chinese herbs, to treat asthma. The typical treatment for asthma attack is a fast-acting inhaler with medication. Sit upright and take slowly with steady breaths. You hold the key to living well with asthma. Trust your health care provider to give you guidance, and take daily responsibility for your breathing with proven ways to take care of yourself. If you are depressed, you are living in the past; if you are anxious, you are living in the future; if you are at peace, you are living in the present.

Head Shepherd
P.O.G.
Loving Ministry

Body

HEALTH/WELLNESS

ASTHMA 2

....

Everyone has eosinophils, a variety of white blood cells that are a normal part of your immune system. But for some people, too many can cause airway inflammation and lead to an asthma attack. Bronchial asthma is a lung disease. Your airways narrow, swell up, and are blocked by excess According to the Asthma and Allergy Foundation of America, as of April 2024, asthma affects more than 27 million people in the U.S. This total includes more than 4.5 million children. Asthma can be life threatening if you don't get treatment. When you breathe normally, the muscles around your airways are relaxed, letting air move easily and quietly. During an asthma attack, three things can happen: 1. Bronchial spasms make the muscles around the airways constrict; 2. The lining of your airways become inflamed; or 3. Mucus production increases, and the thick mucus clogs airways. As your airways get tighter, you make a sound called wheezing. If you're having an asthma attack or other respiratory issues and your breathing aggravates your airways, you might wheeze when you breathe out. You might also hear an asthma attack called an exacerbation or a flare up. Many solutions, useful for when your asthma isn't under control, get credit for being natural asthma remedies, such as acupuncture, biofeedback, plant-based diets, weight loss, caffeine (a mild bronchial dilator that helps open your airways), yoga, etc. As you consider the different types of natural asthma remedies, it's important to carefully balance your desire to breathe easier with the possible dangers of the treatment, which may be unknown. Keep these things in mind. Don't count the days, make the days count.

Head Shepherd
P.O.G.
Loving Ministry

Body

HEALTH/WELLNESS

ASTIGMATISM

Astigmatism is an uneven curvature of the eyes, corneas or lenses. It's a very common eye condition that about one in three Americans have, but it can cause inconvenient vision problems, including blurry vision and poor eyesight at night. It's typically very treatable; often, all you need is a new pair of glasses or contact lenses. Think of your cornea as a clear, round dome over the surface of your eye. In people with astigmatism, that dome is imperfectly round; it's shaped more like an egg or a football. The irregular shape of the cornea affects how light is focused inside the eye. How do you know if you have astigmatism? If you have blurry vision when looking up close or far away; a need to squint to discern objects at any distance; difficulty seeing clearly in the dark, or at night; eye strain or eye discomfort headaches. An optometrist or an ophthalmologist will be able to tell you whether you have astigmatism, and how severe it is. Just remember that if you do end up needing glasses or contacts to help treat astigmatism, you're in good company. Vitamin A or B ais excellent for good eye health. Natural sources of vitamin A include dark leafy vegetables like spinach and kale as well as carrots and winter squash. Vitamin B will encourage good vision also. Fish like salmon, trout, and catfish are an excellent source of Vitamin B. Eggs, poultry, beef, and lamb make a good addition to your meals as well. Including Vitamin A or B in your regular diet will ensure you're getting all the vitamins you need for good vision. Stay focused and you will see life in a wonderful way!

Head Shepherd
P.O.G.
Loving Ministry

HEALTH/WELLNESS
BACK PAIN

....

Job30:17
Night pierces my bones;
my gnawing pains never rest.

Good morning, people of God. Have you ever suffered from severe pain, whether it's in your knees, or your back? I just recently suffered from a back pain that was so excruciating I thought I was never going to walk again. We take so many things for granted, and I learned firsthand what it's like to suffer from pain that a lot of people go through daily. There are some things that you can use to help with pain, like peppermint oil. It gives a cooling sensation and a calming effect on the body, which can relieve sore muscles when used topically. Another thing you can do to relieve pain is drink green tea with lemon, honey, and ginger. Ginger helps reduce pain and inflammation, making it valuable in managing arthritis, headaches, and muscle cramps. It has a warming effect and it stimulates circulation. If you find that the home remedies do not work for you, always follow up with your family doctor to make sure that everything is okay. Remember to pay attention to your body. God says walk in obedience to all that the Lord your God has commanded you, so that you may live and prosper and prolong your days in the land that you will possess.

Lady Shepherd
P.O.G.
Loving Ministry

Body

HEALTH/WELLNESS

BANANAS

....

A typical banana contains about 90 calories and is an excellent source of potassium, vitamin B6, and vitamin C. India is the world's top banana-producing country. Potassium is one of the most important minerals in the body. A diet high in potassium may help reduce blood pressure and water retention, protect against strokes, and prevent osteoporosis and kidney stones. Bananas are a versatile fruit that serve many purposes. Banana sap is used for medicinal purposes in some areas of the world. They are known for the energy boost and potassium increase that takes place through consumption. As a food, they are consumed fresh, dried as a chip, ground into flour, and cooked by grilling, frying, or baking. Bananas are also used in popular dishes such as banana bread, banana cream pie, banana splits, and banana pudding, but bananas also work well blended into soups and left in chunks in curry and stew recipes. Change how you eat to change how you look. The way to get started is to quit talking and begin doing!

Head Shepherd
P.O.G.
Loving Ministry

Body

HEALTH/WELLNESS

BENEFITS OF EATING STRAWBERRIES

Packed with vitamins, fiber, and particularly high levels of antioxidants known as polyphenols, strawberries are a sodium-free, fat-free, cholesterol-free, low-calorie food. They are also a good source of manganese, magnesium, and potassium. Potassium can help lower blood pressure, as it helps buffer the negative effects of sodium and reduce the risk of strokes. Eating strawberries may also reduce your chances of having a heart attack. Regularly eating berries, including strawberries, has been linked to a reduced risk of cancer, including esophageal cancer and lung cancer. Fiber plays an essential role in keeping your gut healthy by feeding it good bacteria. Most Americans don't eat enough, so if you can, add more fiber-rich whole grains, fruits, and veggies to your diet. It can help combat diseases of the gut like cancer and constipation. Almost every family in America enjoys eating strawberries due to their deliciousness. First cultivated in ancient Rome, these fruits have become one of the most popular berries worldwide. The fact that we can heal our bodies through food is the best-kept secret by the medical world. Our health is connected to what we eat, plain and simple. Knowledge is power, but knowledge about yourself is self-empowerment.

Head Shepherd
P.O.G.
Loving Ministry

HEALTH/WELLNESS
BENEFITS OF TURMERIC

A relative of ginger, the vivid yellow orange spice called turmeric is common in Indian, Southeast Asian, and Middle Eastern cooking. It has also been used as a medicine in places like India for centuries to treat issues such as breathing problems. More recently, turmeric has become known as a super food that can fight cancer, ease depression, and more. Turmeric contains curcumin and other chemicals that may decrease swelling and inflammation. Because of this, turmeric might be beneficial for treating conditions that involve inflammation. Additionally, antioxidants in turmeric appear to be so powerful that they may stop your liver from being damaged by toxins. This could be good news for people who take strong drugs for diabetes or other health conditions that may hurt their liver with long-term use. However, when it comes to good health, you are your own doctor. Watch the food you eat and stay hydrated. Get out in nature, take a walk, and breathe in some fresh air. Think of yourself being healthy and whole. It's your mind that keeps you healthy. Your belief system is what connects you to the universal God. He hears you when you ask him for healing, and he will send it your way. Where you place your attention is where your energy flows. Your attitude dictates your vibration; in return, that dictates your life.

Head Shepherd
P.O.G.
Loving Ministry

Body

HEALTH/WELLNESS

BIRTH

....

When we love, we always strive to become better than we are. When we strive to become better than we are, everything around us becomes better too. Who better to love than your own child? Birth is a precious gift from God that keeps humanity moving on. You have been blessed with someone of importance to mold into a spiritual being. For all of its simplicity, nature's plan for birth actually requires a fair amount of flexibility. Each mother and each body are different. While the anatomy and the physiology are standard, how each labor and birth proceeds is fine tuned through the active involvement of the laboring woman. All through labor, her body tells her what is happening, and it helps her discover what she needs to do to help. The involvement of the laboring woman is a crucial piece of nature's plan for birth. The hard work of labor is not meant to be accomplished alone. Changing positions to avoid exhaustion and staying adequately nourished requires assistance, so across the world, women giving birth are supported, encouraged, and comforted by family, friends, and professionals. Giving birth as nature intended is not biting the bullet and letting it happen. Woman know how to give birth without machines or epidurals and fear. Why natural childbirth? The more important question might be, why not? You are not a product of my circumstance, I am a product of my decisions.

Head Shepherd
P.O.G.
Loving Ministry

HEALTH/WELLNESS
BODY BUILDING STRENGTH

....

You must be able to build strength mentally and physically to get through life. Your mind controls your body, telling it how to react. Confidence and accomplishments go hand in hand. Accomplishing goals and even taking small steps toward your goals can help build your self-esteem. Highly confident people tend to live by a value system and make decisions based on their value system, even when it's not necessarily in their best interests. When your decisions are aligned with your highest self, it can cultivate a more confident mind. Exercise not only benefits your physical body, but your mind as well. Mental benefits of exercise include improved focus, memory retention, and stress and anxiety management. Exercise is also said to both prevent and aid depression. Confidence from exercising comes not only from improvements in physical appearance, but also from the mental benefits. Isaiah 41:10 So do not fear, for I am with you; do not be dismayed, for I am your God.

I will strengthen you and help you; I will uphold you with my righteous right hand.

We must all suffer one of two things: the pain of discipline or the pain of regret and disappointment.

Head Shepherd
P.O.G.
Loving Ministry

HEALTH/WELLNESS

BODY FAT

....

Body composition refers to the body's relative percentage of fat, muscle, and water. Understanding their bodies' fat and muscle content can be an important way for people to track their overall health. At present, most weight scales are equipped with special application software that can be connected to our smartphones or tablets so we can easily track our weight and body fat measurement records at any time. Maintaining a trim midsection does more than make you look great – it can also help you live longer. Larger waistlines are linked to a higher risk of heart disease, diabetes, and even cancer. Losing weight, especially belly fat, also improves blood vessel functioning and sleep quality. It's impossible to target belly fat specifcally when you diet, but losing weight overall will help shrink your waistline. More importantly, it will help reduce the dangerous layer of visceral fat, a type of fat within the abdominal cavity that you can't see but heightens health risk. Losing excess body fat, particularly around the belly, can be achieved successfully by consciously incorporating some positive lifestyle modifcations, including following a balanced diet, ample hydration, regular exercise, lowering levels of stress, eating meals on time, avoiding unhealthy food, and consistently monitoring body weight. If you always do what you always done, you'll always get what you've always gotten. Good health isn't luck. It's hard work and dedication.

Head Shepherd
P.O.G.
Loving Ministry

Body

HEALTH/WELLNESS

BLOOD CLOTS

....

Good morning, people of God. I want to tell you all about a situation that happened to a friend of mine. My friend is very active in sports, and she recently had surgery. The surgery caused her to be at risk for a deep vein thrombosis known as a blood clot. They are known to be fatal if you do not take preventative measures. According to the Centers for Disease Control and Prevention, blood clots cause more than 100,000 deaths each year in the United States alone. A blood clot forms when the blood blocks the flow of more blood. At that point, it can be very dangerous, because it can break off and cause a pulmonary embolism. There are several ways to tell if you have a blood clot: if you experience redness, warmth, fever, shortness of breath, dizziness, and/or rapid heart beat. Some ways to prevent blood clots include staying active; continuing to move your body such as by contracting your calf muscles or pointing and moving your toes if you are sitting for a long period of time; or taking blood thinners. Seek the care of a doctor who specializes in peripheral vascular care. God says your body is your temple. Pay attention to the signs of your body. There are always indicators that something is going on.

Lady Shepherd
P.O.G.
Loving Ministry

Body

HEALTH/WELLNESS

BLOOD SUGAR

Our junk food culture promotes blood sugar disorder. The brain needs a steady supply of glucose and cannot adapt well to or compensate for erratic changes in blood sugar levels. This is why symptoms of blood sugar disorders are as varied as many functions of the brain, which is involved in all sensory, motor, perceptual, cognitive, and emotional functions. A brain that is not fed properly becomes unstable. Mercury disrupts the function of the hormone insulin, disables the beta cells of the pancreas, which produces insulin, and disturbs the insulin receptor sites in all the body's cells. Heavy metals, such as arsenic, lead, and aluminum, also disrupt glucose metabolism. Regular exercise is very important for any blood sugar disorder. During exercise, and for several hours afterward, the transport of glucose into the cells is increased due to cells' greater receptivity to insulin. There are ways to lower blood sugar levels naturally. Fiber slows the digestion of carbohydrates and the absorption of sugars, promoting a more gradual rise in blood sugar levels. Drinking enough water may help you keep your blood sugar levels within healthy limits. In addition to preventing dehydration, it helps your kidneys flush out the excess sugar through urine. Try drinking apple cider vinegar mixed in a few ounces of water before a high carb meal. You must believe you're able to be healed through your prayers. The Heavenly Father is waiting for you to ask Him!

Head Shepherd
P.O.G.
Loving Ministry

Body

HEALTH/WELLNESS

BLOOD WORK

Blood tests help doctors check for certain diseases and conditions. They also help check the function of your organs and show how well treatments are working. Specifically, blood tests can help doctors evaluate how well organs such as your kidneys, liver, thyroid, and heart are working. Getting tested at routine intervals can allow you to see the way your body changes over time and empower you to make informed decisions about your health. Knowing levels of various blood components such as HDLs, LDLs, and total cholesterol can allow you to tweak your diet or fitness plan to minimize unhealthy habits that you may not realize are unhealthy and maximize the nutrients you put in your body. Regular blood tests can also catch the warning signs of almost any disease early. Many heart, lung, and kidney conditions can be diagnosed using blood tests. Leviticus 17:11

For the life of a creature is in the blood, and I have given it to you to make atonement for yourselves on the altar; it is the blood that makes atonement for one's life.

May God be your way and light for he is only one who truly cares for you. When you surround yourself with love and the right people, anything is possible.

Head Shepherd
P.O.G.
Loving Ministry

Body

HEALTH/WELLNESS

BURNING FAT

....

One of the most difficult tasks is to step toward your fear. Quit wasting time chasing your passion and do what you're good at. Losing body fat can be a challenging task that requires hard work, patience, and dedication. Many fad diets and fat-burning supplements promise quick results. Modifying your diet, lifestyle, and exercise routine is the most effective way to reach and maintain a healthy weight. Strength training is a type of exercise in which your muscles contract against resistance. It builds muscle mass,increases strength over time, and usually involves lifting weights. Eating more protein rich foods may help reduce your appetite and increase fat burning. Going to bed a bit earlier or setting your alarm clock a little later is a simple strategy to help you reach and maintain a healthy weight. Swapping out sugary drinks for healthier selections is one of the easiest ways to promote long-term, sustainable fat loss. Be sure to pair these simple nutrition tips with a well-rounded diet and active lifestyle to promote long-lasting, sustainable fat burning. 3 John 1:2

Dear friend, I pray that you may enjoy good health and that all may go well with you, even as your soul is getting along well.

Head Shepherd
P.O.G.
Loving Ministry

Body
HEALTH/WELLNESS
CANNED FOODS

Canned foods can be a nutritious option when fresh foods aren't available. They provide essential nutrients and are incredibly convenient. That said, canned foods are also a significant source of Bisphenol A (BPA), which may cause health problems. BPA in canned foods can migrate from the cans into the food they contain. If you're trying to minimize your exposure to BPA, eating a lot of canned food is not the best idea. Some people claim canned foods contain other harmful ingredients as well and should be avoided. Others say canned foods can be a part of a healthy diet. Canning is a method of preserving foods for long periods of time by packing them in airtight containers. The technique was first developed in the late 18th century as a way to provide a stable food source for soldiers and sailors at war. It allows food to be shelf stable and safe to eat for one to five years or longer. It's important to never eat from cans that are bulging, dented, cracked, or leaking. As with all foods, it's important to read the label and ingredient list. By draining and rinsing canned food, you can lower their salt and sugar contents. Canned food can be part of a healthy diet, but it's important to read labels and choose accordingly. Whatever you tolerate will never change!

Head Shepherd
P.O.G.
Loving Ministry

Body

HEALTH/WELLNESS

CHIROPRACTOR

....

While quick chiropractic work does deal with the central nervous system, it's quite different from craniosacral therapy. Chiropractors specialize in realigning the skeletal structure, particularly the spine, to release any nerves that are pinched, or compressed, so that nerve impulses can again flow unimpeded throughout the body. It's amazing what can be accomplished in the hands of a skilled chiropractor. Aside from eliminating pain in your arms, legs, and back, chiropractic therapy can help alleviate many serious conditions, including colitis, sinus infections, and indigestion. Adjustments can even improve poor vision, sharpen reflexes, and restore memory. These apparently magical changes are not mysterious once you realize that all of the nerves governing voluntary and involuntary processes in the body meet at the spine. While some may think you need to be in pain or suffering from a particular condition to benefit from chiropractic care, being proactive in maintaining a healthy spine for preventative measures can be just as valuable to your lifestyle. Chiropractic therapy makes you feel so much better. When I walk out of the clinic, I feel like I'm about three inches taller and everything is in place. As long as I see the chiropractor, I feel like I am one step ahead of the game. Your nervous system is a frequency that connects us all to God.

Head Shepherd
P.O.G.
Loving Ministry

Body

HEALTH/WELLNESS

CONGENITAL INSENSITIVITY TO PAIN

Congenital insensitivity to pain is a condition that inhibits the ability to perceive physical pain. From birth, affected individuals never feel pain in any part of their body when injured. People with this condition can feel the differences between sharp and dull and hot and cold but cannot sense for example that a hot beverage is burning their tongue. The lack of pain awareness often leads to an accumulation of wounds, bruises, broken bones, and other health issues that may go undetected. Young children with congenital insensitivity may have mouth or finger wounds due to repeated self biting and may also experience multiple burns or related injuries. These repeated injuries often lead to reduced life expectancy in people with congenital insensitivity to pain. Many people with congenital insensitivity to pain also have a complete loss of sense of smell, saying they even suffer from peripheral neuropathy. This is because it affects the nervous system, the organ system that connects to the brain and spinal cord, which detect sensation such as touch, smell, and pain. Unfortunately, there is no cure for CIP or treatment aside from patient education, which includes teaching patients how to avoid injuries and get treatment as soon as possible.

Head Shepherd
P.O.G.
Loving Ministry

Body

HEALTH/WELLNESS

CONGESTION

Chest congestion is the accumulation of mucus in the lungs and the lower breathing tubes. It is usually accompanied by a wet, productive cough that brings up thick mucus. Chest congestion may cause you to hear or feel wheezing or crackling sounds when you breathe in and out. Infection with the cold or flu virus is among the most common causes of chest congestion and happens when the infection progresses from the upper respiratory tract into your nasal passage, sinuses, and throat into your lower respiratory tract, breathing tubes, and lungs. Your body tries to remove packages by generating mucus to trap them and prevent them from reaching the cells that line your lungs and airways. Then, the sweeping action of tiny hairlike particles that line your lower respiratory tract called cilia help move the mucus, along with the irritants, up and out of your lungs and breathing passages. The presence of the mucus also triggers nerve sensors that make you cough, which further facilitates the removal of the excess mucus, triggering a wet chest cough. Some home remedies like lemon juice, honey, ginger syrup with cinnamon, or peppermint tea contain substances with antiinflammatory, antiseptic, and antioxidant action. To prepare, place one teaspoon of echinacea root or leaves into the cup of boiling water; allow to soak for 15 minutes; strain; and drink twice per day. Accept responsibility for your life. Know that it is you, no one else, who will get you where you want to go.

Head Shepherd
P.O.G.
Loving Ministry

Body
HEALTH/WELLNESS
CONSTIPATION

2 Chronicles 21:15

You yourself will be very ill with a lingering disease of the bowels, until the disease causes your bowels to come out. Good morning, P.O.G. family. Do you ever feel bloated or uncomfortable after eating a meal? Do you feel like your food is not digesting well? Or are you having a hard time passing stool? You, my friend, are constipated. I have some home remedies that can help with that: 1. Drink milk and almond oil in the morning on an empty stomach and at bedtime. It will cure constipation quickly. 2. Add 50 milliliters of spinach juice and one teaspoon of fresh lemon juice to one glass of carrot juice. Mix well and drink once per day. 3. Banana milk is rich in dietary fiber, and it cures constipation and piles. 4. Snake cucumber strengthens the digestive system and cures constipation as well as dehydration. 5. Eating an apple a day also helps with constipation. It is important to have a bowel movement at least twice per day to keep all the toxins out of your body. Anyone who is 50 and over should have a colonoscopy. Remember when you go this will help you to keep going.

Lady Shepherd
P.O.G.
Loving Ministry

Body

HEALTH/WELLNESS
CORTISONE

....

Have you ever been in so much pain that you can barely walk or stretch out? Have you ever been in so much pain that you have to think before you move? You had to really set your mind up to move around. You couldn't even perform what once came to you naturally, like walking or stretching. Just getting up and moving around was a challenge. Your knees were so swollen with so much fluid in your joints that you had to get fluid aspirated from your knees and get a cortisone injection. It's actually called a hydrocortisone shot, an injection used to treat swollen or painful joints, caused by an injury or arthritis in the knees. The hydrocortisone is injected directly into the painful joint. This is called an intra-articular injection. The joints most often injected are the shoulders, elbows, knees, hands, wrists, and hips. The injection lasts for anywhere from six weeks to six months. The injection provides pain relief by reducing inflammation. Sometimes it can take up to seven days for the cortisone injection to begin to work in the body. The most common side effect is intense pain and swelling in the joints where the injection was given. This usually gets better in a day or two. Just put an ice pack on the injected area. After a few days, you will feel much better and be able to move around and be yourself again. You must crawl before you walk, and walk before you run. Don't ever let any disability keep you from moving forward in life.

Head Shepherd
P.O.G.
Loving Ministry

Body
HEALTH/WELLNESS
CORTISONE INJECTIONS

Good morning, people of God. The other day, the head shepherd was having problems with his left knee. So, we scheduled an appointment with an orthopedic specialist, and the doctor stated that he can drain the fluid from his knee with a needle. At first, the thought of it was frightening, but he was already in pain so he thought he might as well get the cortisone shot. Cortisone is the strongest anti-inflammatory agent available, used to decrease pain and reduce localized swelling. A cortisone injection is similar to taking an anti-inflammatory by mouth (Advil or aspirin) and injecting it locally through a needle directly into joints. I am not going to lie, it takes a few days to get back to normal. Depending on your situation, you still need to exercise and keep moving around. Going to the gym and swimming, biking, or using the elliptical are good ways to exercise your knees. Also, change your diet. Eat vegetables, and watch your alcohol intake; having arthritis and drinking alcohol is not a good combination. Alcohol has yeast in it, and if you have arthritis, it is not good to over-indulge. I know people tell you that arthritis is hereditary, but stop and think for a moment: we eat and drink the same way our parents did. But if we change our behavior, we can change our health. If the pain is too unbearable, call on your Heavenly Father.

Lady Shepherd
P.O.G
Loving Ministry

Body

HEALTH/WELLNESS

COUGH

Is a persistent cough keeping you up at night causing you to have a tight chest or mucus backup? Seasonal allergies, the flu virus, or some kind of lung infection are the most common reasons for a nagging cough. However, a cough can sometimes indicate a more serious health condition, such as asthma. Whatever the reason for your hacking, a cough is the body's typical reflex when foreign material is blocking the upper airway passages of the lungs. So how do you determine one cause from another? Let's take a look at why a cough occurs, and the most common health conditions a cough indicates depending on the associated symptoms. Post nasal drip is a very common source of the itchy, scratchy cough that you get with seasonal allergies. Those with allergies commonly experience post nasal drip during periods of high pollen, such as ragweed season in the late summer and early fall. Here we've listed a few home remedies to consider. You can create your own remedy at home by mixing up to two teaspoons of honey with herbal tea, or water, and lemon. The honey does the soothing while lemon juice can help you with congestion. You can also simply eat the honey by the spoonful or spread it on bread for a snack. You can also benefit by drinking peppermint tea or by inhaling a teaspoon of mint vapors from a steam bath. To make a steam bath, add three or four drops of peppermint oil for every five ounces of hot water. Drape a towel over your head and take deep breaths directly above the water. In the end, believe, and you will receive healing.

Head Shepherd
P.O.G.
Loving Ministry

Body

HEALTH/WELLNESS

DEALING WITH PAIN

....

Novelist George Eliot once said, "It is never too late to be what you might have been." Body aches are an uncomfortable but common symptom of a variety of medical ailments. If you're experiencing body aches, your muscles may feel weak, sore, tired, or hard to move. Luckily, most body aches are easily treatable. A few days of rest and hydration can provide relief from any discomfort. However, some body aches, particularly those that last a long time, can indicate a serious underlying medical condition that may require treatment. Body aches are caused by muscle inflammation. Sometimes body aches can be sharp and intermittent, while in other instances, they may feel more like a prolonged dull, generalized ache. Pains and fatigue are common complaints practically everyone has on occasion. While over-the-counter medications can provide temporary relief, overuse of pain relievers can cause unwanted side effects such as stomach upset. Body aches and muscle pain may have many causes, such as arthritis, bursitis, tendinitis, or fibromyalgia. There are several natural home remedies you can try for these conditions as well as many others. Turmeric is a distinctively flavored spice that's commonly used in Indian cooking. Heat therapy helps to alleviate pain by opening up constricted blood vessels that increase blood flow, which is helpful for reducing joint stiffness. Cold therapy by using ice alleviates the inflammation. Massage therapy helps with the pain as well. If you're under stress or feeling anxious, you may tense up your muscles, causing them to spasm. A positive mindset leads to positive results and a healthy body!

Head Shepherd
P.O.G.
Loving Ministry

Body

HEALTH/WELLNESS

DEHYDRATION

....

Water is essential for the cells and organs in our bodies to function, allowing us to engage in complex activities, such as playing sports, and even processes we don't think about, such as breathing. When we drink enough water, we feel good, our muscles cramp up less when we exercise, our brains perform faster cognitive calculations, and we digest our food more efciently and efectively. Water is critical to our health; after all, the human body is composed of 60% water. In order to achieve greatness, you must frst believe you can. People at any age can become dehydrated, and since younger children and infants might not be able to vocalize or recognize when they are thirsty, it is important to take note of the various symptoms attributed with dehydration. When humans feel thirsty, they are already dehydrated, so the ability to recognize other associated symptoms may help you rehydrate sooner. Signs of dehydration include muscle fatigue, dizziness, thirst, and dry mouth. Since the body is already dehydrated when it is thirsty, it is important to remember to be drinking 64 ounces of water throughout the day even when we do not think we need it. You have to decide what's more important to you: that feeling of reaching the top of the mountain, or the feeling of its shade at the bottom.

Head Shepherd
P.O.G.
Loving Ministry

Body

HEALTH/WELLNESS

DIABETES

There are over half a billion diabetics in the world today. Diabetes occurs when your immune system, the body's system for fighting infection, attacks and destroys the insulin-producing beta cells of the pancreas. Scientists think diabetes is caused by genes and environmental factors, such as viruses. Red meat and processed red meat are both linked to diabetes. Processed meats like bacon, hot dogs, and deli meat are particularly harmful because of their high levels of sodium and nitrates. Some people consider fatty fish to be one of the healthiest food on the planet. Leafy green vegetables are extremely nutritious and low in calories. Drinks such as water, chocolate milk, sweet tea, and orange juice are good for diabetics. Glutathione in some vegetables are good for your cells and help with diabetes. Limit the number of toxins that you come into contact with. Exercise daily. Be consistent and disciplined; then, you will live a fit life.

Head Shepherd
P.O.G.
Loving Ministry

Body

HEALTH/WELLNESS

DKA

....

When it comes to diabetic ketoacidosis (DKA), there is nothing in those 10 syllables that hints at good times or optional outcomes, nor should there be; DKA is serious business, often leading to hospital admissions, intensive care unit stays, or even death. DKA is a life-threatening condition in which ketone numbers rise to dangerous levels in the blood. The body has a way of letting glucose into its cells. There is a door between the cell and the blood, and insulin is the key that opens that door. Insulin allows the cells to recognize the glucose and use it as a fuel source. If you don't have insulin, glucose can't get into the cell. It's like being outside your house without a key to get in. So, there could be a lot of glucose out in the blood, but inside the cell, it does not appear that there is. Naturally, this impacts people with type one diabetes to a greater degree, because they have no insulin, as opposed to type two, where there is merely an insulin deficiency. While most of your body can find alternative fuel sources, the brain cells are picked here. The only two fuel sources they will let in are glucose and ketones. Therefore, when the lack of insulin hides the presence of glucose, the body generates ketones as an effort to feed the brain. The problem is that as more ketones are generated, the pH of the blood starts going down, causing the blood to become more acidic. Ketones can be toxic and high levels can poison the body. To help reduce how often DKA episodes occur and the damage they can cause, Abbott developed continuous glucose monitors. According to Abbott's website, their FreeStyle Libre 2, which provides glucose measurements every minute, is the longest-lasting integrated continuous glucose monitor currently available.

Head Shepherd
P.O.G.
Loving Ministry

HEALTH/WELLNESS
DO THE BEST YOU CAN!

Greatness is not achieved in one giant leap, but in the accumulation of little steps. Every mistake is an opportunity to learn and grow. With perseverance and a desire to inspire and encourage, the ladder of greatness can be climbed. True commitment is born when your vision becomes crystal clear and the value it brings to others becomes your driving force. With a vivid mental picture of your desired outcome, failure is practically impossible. Embrace this vision daily, and you will unlock the power of your subconscious to guide you towards well-being. Losing weight, getting healthier, and overcoming sickness is all up to your thoughts. Your mind is a powerful tool that can bring healing into your life. Being an optimist means looking at the bright side of things. If you keep a positive attitude, you can reduce your stress and improve your outlook on life. If you catch yourself thinking something negative, challenge it with a positive thought. If you catch yourself thinking, *I've never done this before,* replace it with, *This is a good opportunity to learn.* Whenever you want to change the situation you are going through, just change it to something positive. Your mind is a highly programmed database. In short, live your life to be something great.

Head Shepherd
P.O.G.
Loving Ministry

Body

HEALTH/WELLNESS

EATING

....

Don't limit yourself. Many people limit themselves to what they think they can do. You can go as far as your mind lets you. In life, you can achieve what you believe. Eating a healthy balanced diet is one of the most important things you can do to protect your health. Up to 80% of premature heart disease and stroke can be prevented through your life choices, including habits such as eating a healthy diet and being physically active. Courage isn't having the strength to go on. It is going on when you don't have strength. Eating right doesn't have to be complicated. Start building a healthy plate by choosing fruits and vegetables, whole grains, lean protein, and low-fat dairy foods that are packed with the nutrients you need without too many added sugars, fats, and salt. It's hard to resist junk-food-filled vending machines when your stomach is growling at 3 PM, but you don't need to rely on willpower alone. The right food choices earlier in the day can set you up for success. Reach for protein. It fills you up and helps you feel satisfied longer than carbs do. Go for meals and snacks that include things like hard boiled eggs, Greek yogurt, peanut butter, and skinless chicken.

Head Shepherd
P.O.G
Loving Ministry

HEALTH/WELLNESS

EFFECTS OF ALCOHOL

The consumption of ethanol, alcohol, beer, wine, and hard liquor that, among other symptoms, causes edema of the brain tissue, abnormal respiration, impaired judgment, incoherent speech, lack of muscular coordination, and depression. Alcohol consumption often leads to antisocial behavior ranging from drunk driving to interpersonal violence, but alcoholism is more than a behavioral, social, or emotional problem. It reflects and causes imbalance of the brain. The high you feel when drinking is from neurological impairment. Alcohol also causes nutritional deficiencies, which, in turn, can cause alcohol addiction. Sugar is metabolized poorly, which may indicate hypoglycemia or diabetes, making the person crave alcohol to restore blood sugar levels. Thus, alcoholism can be regarded as an addiction to rapidly metabolize sugars and carbohydrates in the form of alcohol. Drinking is also largely accepted as a social activity in a way to cope with stress, even as a potential remedy for insomnia or anxiety. Moderation management is just one alternative to full sobriety; it focuses on reducing alcohol use with an emphasis on finding the best approach for your situation, not anyone else's. Whatever makes you the strongest, pursue that path. Adventure doesn't come if you sleep. You must get up, and follow your heart. That is, aim to achieve your destiny.

Head Shepherd
P.O.G.
Loving Ministry

Body

HEALTH/WELLNESS

EXERCISE

....

Before high rises, cars, and elevators, our ancestors walked, trotted, and ran. They chased the food they hunted, and climbed to reach what they picked. Humans didn't sit for most of the day, slumped over their desks. They didn't ruin their eyes gazing at computers and playing video games, nor did they need to walk on a treadmill or climb the moving stairs at the local gym or health club in order to meet their daily exercise quota. Indeed, these are strange times in which to be alive. Although not everyone lives in the city today, often even country dwellers don't get enough exercise. According to the American Diabetes Association, as of 2021, either diabetes or a pre-diabetic condition affect nearly 41% of the population in the United States. Also, according to the Food Research and Action Center, in the U.S., over 70% of adults are overweight or obese, and over 33% of children are overweight or obese. Can you think of a better time to begin an exercise program? If you want something, go get it; you can do whatever you want, and you can be whatever you want. Do not allow anything negative to control you. Sometimes, we feel like we are slaves to our addictions. If there's a will, there's a way. Never give up, and one day you will reach your goal.

Head Shepherd
P.O.G.
Loving Ministry

HEALTH/WELLNESS

FAKE FOOD

....

If you are not willing to risk the unusual, you will have to settle for the ordinary. There are so many brands of food out there. You have to know what is healthy and what is not. Lots of fast food restaurants have food on their menu that is not nutritious to eat. The food has been created in laboratories. It was not grown by Mother Earth. Even chicken is fake food in some places. Just read the label, and see if you can understand the words. With all the organic and natural options at the grocery store these days, you probably assume you know what's going in your cart. But guess what? It's pretty much a guarantee that something you're buying isn't what you think it is. It could be anything from passing off cheap fish as a more expensive type to diluting an item. And pay attention because some of the sneaky substitutions can make you seriously sick. GMOs are omnipresent in our food supply today. They are the result of a laboratory process with genes from the DNA of one species of bacteria, viruses, animals, or plants that are extracted and artificially implanted into the genes of an unrelated plant or animal. The Grocery Manufacturers Association estimates that they are found in 75 to 80% of the foods in the United States due to their many derivatives. So whether you eat, or drink, or whatever you do, do all to the glory of God

Head Shepherd.
P.O.G.
Loving Ministry

Body

HEALTH/WELLNESS
FASTING GOALS

....

Remember, the moment you accept total responsibility is the moment you claim the power to change everything in your life. Fasting cleanses our body of toxins and forces cells into a process that is not usually stimulated when a steady stream of fuel from food is always present. When we fast, the body does not have its usual access to glucose, forcing the cells to resort to other means and materials to produce energy. Fasting has been practiced for centuries, but can it really help you lose weight and get healthier? How does fasting remove toxins from your body? When you go without eating for more than a day or two, the body enters ketosis. Ketosis occurs when the body runs out of carbohydrates to burn for energy, so it burns fat, and the fat is where the body stores many of the toxins it absorbs from the environment. Fasting has been used for religious and spiritual purification for centuries. Nearly every religious text, from the Old and New Testaments of the Bible to the Koran and the Upanishads, calls upon followers to fast periodically as a rite of spiritual purification, penitence, or preparation for union with God. Matthew 6:18 It will not be obvious to others that you are fasting, but only to your Father, who is unseen; and your Father, who sees what is done in secret, will reward you.

Head Shepherd
P.O.G.
Loving Ministry

Body
HEALTH/WELLNESS
FEELING GOOD

The law of attraction states that whatever you focus on, think about, read about, and talk about intensely, you're going to attract into your life. Feeling good may also improve and promote a range of lifestyle habits that are important for your overall health. People with otherwise healthy lifestyles tend to eat healthier diets with higher intake of fruits, vegetables, and whole grains; in fact, those with a positive well being were 47% more likely to consume fresh fruits, and vegetables then their less positive counterparts. Diets rich in fruits and vegetables have consistently been associated with a range of health benefits, including a lower risk of diabetes, strokes, and heart disease. Regular physical activity helps build strong bones, increase energy levels, decrease body fat, and lower blood pressure. Feeling good may also improve sleep habits and practices, which is important for concentration, productivity, exercise performance, and maintaining a healthy weight. Romans 15:13 May the God of hope fill you with all joy and peace as you trust in him, so that you may overflow with hope by the power of the Holy Spirit. If you want to make a permanent change, stop focusing on the size of your problems, and start focusing on the size of your God.

Head Shepherd
P.O.G.
Loving Ministry

Body

HEALTH/WELLNESS

FIGHTING FAIR

....

1 Timothy 6:12

Fight the good fight of the faith. Take hold of the eternal life to which you were called when you made your good confession in the presence of many witnesses.

Good morning, people of God. Have you ever been in a situation where you are having a good day, and one person who is close to you says something so disrespectful it just hurts your feelings? Or you're dealing with someone who has no filter, and they just say anything that comes to mind? Like you know they are like that, but they say something that does not need to be said at that time? Some people just need to learn how to fight fair. First, you must maintain control. When you don't, your heart starts pounding, and your palms get sweaty. Then, your blood begins to leave the part of your brain that regulates emotional control. The next thing you know, you're flooded with distress. So, take some time out so that you can cool off. Most importantly, let one another have time to speak without interruption and lashing out; just listen and give each other enough time to express how you are feeling. Lastly, say you're sorry, acknowledge the hurt you caused, accept responsibility for it, and ask for forgiveness. I know this is hard. Forgiveness is the best medicine you can have. Once you forgive, you can release all the pain.

Lady Shepherd
P.O.G.
Loving Ministry

Body

HEALTH/WELLNESS

FLU

....

In 2005, U.S. President George W. Bush predicted that two hundred thousand to over two million people in the U.S. alone would die from the avian flu. These figures were doubtfully reported in the press despite the fact that up to that point only 60 deaths from the flu had been reported. The flu is a common viral infection that attacks the lungs, nose, and throat and can be deadly, especially for high-risk groups. Young children, older adults, pregnant women, and other people with chronic diseases or weak immune systems are at high risk. When cold and flu season comes around, it's easy to get overwhelmed. Thankfully, there's a simple choice. Florida orange juice is full of essential nutrients like vitamin C, potassium, and folate, which help to support your immune system and keep you hydrated. Doctors say that the alcohol in Lysol enhances sanitization, but sometimes the old ways are the best ways – in this case, those are washing your hands with soap and warm water for 60 seconds. There are only 4 seasons, and flu season does not have to be one of them. Flu viruses commonly circulate during the winter when people are inside getting less sunlight, dealing with stress and indulging in more food as associated with the holidays. Our immune system is designed to fight off pathogens and attacks the things we encounter in the world that makes us sick. Vitamin D or sunlight will help with immune functioning as well. Stay healthy, stay whole, and pray.

Head Shepherd
P.O.G.
Loving Ministry

Body

HEALTH/WELLNESS

FRESH AIR

....

Similar to the way fresh air works to provide energy, the smell and intake of oxygen allows you to feel better overall. Getting fresh air on a regular basis can help fight depression or feelings of worthlessness. It also helps that getting fresh air often means getting a blast of vitamin D as well. If you've ever been stuck inside for days on end, you know how boring and depressing it can be. While it's easy to think that this boredom is simply caused by a lack of something to do, it might be that you need a breath of fresh air. As people have known for a long time, fresh air is really good for our health, but why? What's the big deal about getting outdoors? Take a look at these three great reasons to schedule some time in the Sun and fresh air today. It has been proven time and time again that a blast of fresh air can actually give you more energy. If you're feeling run down or fatigued, go for a quick walk in the great outdoors. The oxygen along with the smells of nature, such as the trees, the flowers, and the rain, help to increase your energy levels as well as your awareness. You may find that you feel more awake and alert If you spend a few minutes outside every day. Fresh air can really lift your spirits. The bottom line: if you're in a funk, step outside to get back on track.

Head Shepherd
P.O.G.
Loving Ministry

Body

HEALTH/WELLNESS

FUEL YOUR VESSEL

What makes you feel low in energy? Many factors infuence your energy levels, but some lifestyle factors have a greater impact than others. The best way to refuel your body is to expose yourself to sunlight. When you begin to feel cabin fever, take a walk outside. From promoting the growth of plants and crops to keeping people warm, sunlight is essential for life. Many people enjoy the feeling of sunlight, and there is increasing evidence to support its many health benefts. Of all the health benefts of being out in the sunlight, producing vitamin D in the Body is one of the best known. Exposure to the sun is linked to lowering blood pressure levels and reducing death rates from cardiovascular issues. It also triggers the release of stores of nitrogen oxide, which causes arteries to dilate, lowering blood pressure and possibly reducing the impact of metabolic syndrome. Additionally, sunlight supports better sleep and regulates circadian rhythms by monitoring serotonin and melatonin levels. Being in the sun generally makes people feel better. Sunlight exposure aside, scientists have found that low energy often occurs as a result of what you eat. Refuel your body by eating high quality carbohydrates like whole grains, fruits, and vegetables; lean protein sources such as lean cuts of meat, poultry, low fat milk, and beans; and healthy fats from sources like nuts, olive oil, and avocados. It depends how you would like to recharge. In the end, just do it!

Head Shepherd
P.O.G.
Loving Ministry

Body

HEALTH/WELLNESS

GOING TO THE DOCTOR

Mark 2:17

On hearing this, Jesus said to them, "It is not the healthy who need a doctor, but the sick. I have not come to call the righteous, but sinners."

Good morning, people of God. Do you have something going on with your body, and you are wondering what is going on? But you don't want to alarm anyone, so, you just figure if you endure it, it will go away. Are you having any unexplained weight loss, or your heart has been beating really fast, or you keep losing your breath? Or do you have any other symptoms that you are silently suffering from that you don't want anybody to know about? Well, my friend, it is time for you to go to the doctor and get yourself checked out. If you drive a vehicle, you know that before winter comes around, you will need to change your oil and get a tuneup. The same thing goes for your body. I know it is expensive going to the doctor, but don't you think you're worth it? Preventative maintenance is a beautiful thing. God says your body is your temple. We should treat it as such, and take better care of ourselves. You know your body. Don't ignore the signs. Even though it's scary, it's worth it. Spare your loved ones of the costly demise of yourself, or the high cost of an emergency room. There is affordable healthcare. If you're not working, there are county hospitals and agencies that will help with the cost of preventative medicine. Don't worry about the cost of taking care of yourself, because with your Father, all things are possible.

Lady Shepherd
P.O.G.
Loving Ministry

Body

HEALTH/WELLNESS

GUT HEALTH!

Your digestive system plays an important part in the health of your body. That is why you should defecate each time after you have eaten something. Otherwise, the preservatives and toxins in the food we eat will cause health problems for the body. We need to try and consume foods with less preservatives in them. A good start will be not to use canned food in your diet. Symptoms of a bad gut include gas, bloating, acid reflux, abdominal pain, and constipation. According to a survey by Fox News in 2013, 74% of Americans are living with digestive issues. A bad gut can be caused by problems like anxiety, depression, insomnia, migraine headaches, itchy eyes, arthritis, liver disease, and a dozen other conditions. To improve your gut health, it's important to get enough sleep, eat slowly, stay hydrated, and take a probiotic. We realize that the healthy balance of our gut health helps keep us in balance with our physical health, our immunity, and even other mental health. Inflammation and high stress can cause a bad gut as well. Try some natural ways to try to lower stress, such as meditation, yoga, essential oils, massage, or decreasing caffeine intake. You can also try reflexology. Reflexology helps with your digestive tract by using a finger work walking technique through the small intestines, clearing any blockage in the process, in waking up the body digestion. Reflexology is a natural digestive aid that stimulates all components of the digestive system and encourages its parts to work in better harmony with each other. Its relaxing abilities allow your internal organs to breathe and be able to work. There are lots of things that you can do naturally to help your digestive system.

Lady Shepherd
P.O.G.
Loving Ministry

HEALTH/WELLNESS

HEADACHES

....

M ost of us get headaches from time to time. Some are mild, while others cause throbbing pain. They can last for a minute or days. There are many different types of headaches. How you treat yours depends on which kind you have. Headaches might arise because of another medical condition such as swollen sinuses or a head injury. In these cases, treating the underlying problem usually relieves the headache as well. But most headaches, including tension headaches and migraines, aren't caused by a separate illness. A headache may feel like a pain inside of your brain, but it's not. Most headaches begin in the many nerves of the muscles and blood vessels that surround your head, neck, and face. These pain-sensing nerves can be set off by stress, muscle tension, enlarged blood vessels, and other triggers. Once activated, the nerves send messages to the brain, and it can feel like the pain is coming from deep within your head. Lifestyle changes to relax and reduce stress might help, such as yoga, stretching, massages, and other tension relievers. Magnesium is one of the most successful headache remedies. First of all, because it's much safer than taking a painkiller. People who suffer from serious headaches like migraines often have low levels of magnesium, and several studies suggest that magnesium may reduced the frequency of migraine attacks in people with low levels. Dairy products, meats, chocolate, and coffee include decent levels of magnesium. Don't be pushed around by the fears in your mind, be led by the dreams in your heart. You will accomplish everything you set your mind to! Just take the steps needed.

Head Shepherd
P.O.G.
Loving Ministry

Body

HEALTH/WELLNESS

HEALTH PROGRAM

....

Remember, you will never find true success. In uncomfortable situations, push yourself, and push your limits. Healthy movement may include walking, sports, dancing, yoga, running, or other activities you enjoy. Eat a well-balanced, low fat diet with lots of fruits, vegetables, and whole grains. Choose a diet that's low in saturated fat and cholesterol and moderate in sugar, salt, and total fat. Good health can decrease your risk of developing certain diseases and conditions. These include heart disease, strokes, some cancers, and injuries. Routine exercise can make you feel better and keep your weight under control. Try to be active for 30 to 60 minutes about five times per week. Any amount of exercise is better than none. You were created on purpose with the purpose to manifest that purpose through you. Meditation helps prevent age-related changes in the brain. Try your best to sit in a quiet place with your eyes closed, relaxed, your jaw and shoulders connected to your breath, your mind empty, and stay in the present moment for 10 to 20 minutes each day. If you have not tried meditation before, there are several guided meditation videos online and books on meditation at your local library. Life can be tough at times, but it's important to remember that we have the strength and determination to overcome our health problems and obstacles that come our way. Instead of letting setbacks deflect us from our goals, we can use them as a springboard to become even stronger and more resilient. So, keep pushing forward. Stay positive and never give up on your health. With the right mindset, you can achieve anything you set your mind to.

Head Shepherd
P.O.G.
Loving Ministry

Body

HEALTH/WELLNESS

HEALTHY LIVING

Many people think that being healthy is a difficult task that involves lots of dieting and time at the gym, but that's not actually true. By making some simple tweaks to your routine and setting small goals for yourself, you can be on the path towards living a healthier, happier life. Start a daily habit of making healthier choices when it comes to eating, relaxing, being active, and sleeping. Soon, you'll start to see your healthy life taking shape. Sugary, sweetened beverages are also uniquely harmful for children as they can contribute not only to obesity in children but also to conditions that usually do not develop until well into adulthood, such as type 2 diabetes and high blood pressure. Some people avoid nuts because they are high in fat. However, nuts and seeds are incredibly nutritious. They are packed with protein, fiber, and a variety of vitamins and minerals. Nuts may help you lose weight and reduce your risk of developing type 2 diabetes and heart disease. God is saying to you today, "What you have been praying for is about to happen for you. You've passed the test, you have learned the lesson. You've been patient, you will remain strong through many trials and challenges. Nothing broke you. You're still here, standing strong. Now is the time for you to start receiving blessings, healing, and happiness. Life is tough, so you have to be strong."

Head Shepherd
P.O.G.
Loving Ministry

Body

HEALTH/WELLNESS

HEALTHY MOUTH

Proper oral hygiene is essential for healthy teeth and gums. This includes daily brushing and flossing. In addition, you should see your dentist regularly for dental exams and cleaning. Preventative dentistry gives you the best chance for a beautiful smile and long-lasting oral health. Oral health is also linked to whole body health; if an infection is present in your mouth, your bloodstream can carry the bacteria to other areas of your body, leading to much more serious health concerns like heart disease and strokes. Keeping your teeth and gums healthy is an important part of long-lasting overall health. Also, excellent oral hygiene protects your teeth and gums and keeps your smile beautiful. Here are our home remedies to keep your oral cavity in terrific shape and avoid dental disasters. 1. Vitamins are a powerful source of nutrition and vitamin C is a strong antioxidant that can keep your gums healthy and your teeth strong. Do you love cranberries? You are in luck, as cranberry juice is a huge aid in preventing cavities. There is a compound in cranberries that helps to disarm the pathogens causing decay in your teeth. 2. Next time you make your favorite pizza, try putting cloves on it or maybe sprinkle your pasta with some of this delicious spice. Not only do cloves smell amazing and taste good, but they keep cavities from spreading and can alleviate pain. 3. Take some of that vegetable or coconut oil from your pantry and rinse your mouth with it to prevent cavities from decaying and decrease swollen gums. Rinsing your mouth with one of these oils from about 10 minutes will pull bacteria away from your mouth. Even though I hurt, I smile. I know God is working, so I smile.

Head Shepherd
P.O.G.
Loving Ministry

HEALTH/WELLNESS
HEARTBURN

What is heartburn, and what causes it? Heartburn occurs when acid from the stomach rises to the soft esophagus, causing a burning sensation. This can be caused by an abnormally positioned stomach, which needs to be forced back into place either by a chiropractor trained in the technique, or someone else including you, although it's harder to do this on your own body. Another cause can be an insufficient supply of hydrochloric acid in the stomach. This results in the fermentation of undigested food, causing solids and fumes to rise. Try nutritional supplements, such as digestive enzymes with supplemental hydrochloric acid, or herbs, including turmeric, fennel, ginger, and milk thistle to stimulate stomach secretion and bile flow. Avoid lying down for at least three hours after a meal. Lying down after eating could cause stomach acid to rise, leading to heartburn and indigestion. Additionally, try not to eat before bedtime, and consider raising the head of your bed in order to keep your head and shoulders elevated. You can keep your body fit by exercising and meditating more. We need peace of mind, not more food before bedtime. Take time to love yourself, then show love to others. God will do the rest when you ask him to.

Head Shepherd
P.O.G.
Loving Ministry

Body
HEALTH/WELLNESS
HEART

You must develop extreme confidence so that you have the ability to ignore the opinions of negative people. You can do it if you think you can. The cardiovascular system consists of the heart valves and blood vessels. The heart is a pear-shaped organ in the chest between the lungs that leans toward the left. Arteries carry blood away from the heart and pick up oxygen from the lungs. They become tiny capillaries that carry the oxygen-rich red blood to every cell in the body. At the point that the arterial capillaries pick up carbon dioxide from the cells, they are called venous capillaries, which then become the veins that carry the now blue-tinted blood back to the heart. The veins deposit the carbon dioxide into the lungs just before the venous blood returns to the heart to be recirculated through the body. This very complex pump consisting of four chambers contains valves that regulate the blood as it flows through. Although the heart is classified as an organ, it is also considered an involuntary muscle. If you want to keep your heart healthy, you'll typically do three things: choose nutritious foods, stay active, and toss bad habits like smoking. Garlic has been used for centuries to boost heart health as well as other things. If you want to know more about heart health, do your own research to learn more.

Head Shepherd
P.O.G.
Loving Ministry

HEALTH/WELLNESS

HEAVY METALS

....

Your body is where your soul is, so you must take care of your body. What you feed your system is very important. For years, the enemy has been trying to destroy this structure. The term "heavy metal" refers to any metallic chemical element that has a relatively high density and is toxic or poisonous at low concentration, like mercury, chromium, lead and aluminum. These are found in the shot the enemy wants you to take. This will change your DNA and make you sick. These rulers have been poisoning us for years. The air we breathe, the food that we consume, and the water we drink are not even safe. There are many toxins in our environment, so we have to be careful what we choose to eat. The body's immune system can only fight off one virus at a time. We must help it out by watching what we feed our body. Take time to find out what type of ingredients are in the food you buy and the medicine you take. In order to change your life, first change your diet. The enemy knows that he can keep us sick and we will not have the energy to fight off his injust ways. These are some nutritious ways to detox metals from the body. Eat garlic, cilantro, or wild blueberries or drink lemon water. There are other ways, but you have to do your own research. You need to be healthy to live your best life now. Your belief also has an impact on your life. We have to not let any negative thoughts about our health enter our mind. Listen to music tuned to 432 Hz to relax you when you're alone. Meditate about your body being free of sickness and disease; God will hear you and heal your body when you believe!

Head Shepherd
P.O.G
Loving Ministry

Body
HEALTH/WELLNESS
HERBS

When you hear the word "herb", it's easy to think about the oregano in your mom's spaghetti sauce and forget the centuries during which humankind used herbs as medicine in thousands of ways. How did our ancestors know which plant to use for what ailed them? They observe what plants sick animals ate to find new remedies. The most experienced herbalists or medicine men roamed the outdoors with their followers. When they saw an interesting new plant, they stopped to smell, picked it, ate it, and waited to see what the effects were. As you might imagine, this method produced some casualties. Through centuries of observation, treatment, and experimentation, humans learn which herbs worked, and under what circumstances. Knowledge was first imparted orally, and later, carefully written records were kept. As one of the oldest tree spices, ginkgo is also one of the oldest homeopathic plants and a key herb in Chinese medicine. The leaves are used to create capsules, tablets, and extracts; when dried, it can also be consumed as tea. It's perhaps best known for its ability to boost brain health. Originating in India, another herb called turmeric is believed to have anti-cancer properties and can prevent DNA mutation. As an anti-inflammatory, it can be taken as a supplement and has been used topically for people with arthritis who wish to relieve discomfort. There are lots of herbs for different elements. Do your research to see which one works best for you.

Head Shepherd
P.O.G.
Loving Ministry

HEALTH/WELLNESS

HEREDITARY

Romans 5:12

Therefore, just as sin entered the world through one man, and death through sin, and in this way death came to all people, because we all sinned–

Good morning, people of God. Do you ever wonder why you do or say certain things? It is a learned behavior from your parents, and your parents learned it from their parents. It has been in your generation for so long it is called hereditary. Hereditary means the passing of physical or mental characteristics genetically from one generation to another. For instance, if your grandfather has diabetes, cancer, or high blood pressure, some of your other family members may have it also. Studies show that some of these diseases come from bad eating habits and lack of exercise. We like our chitterlings, hog maws, and sweet desserts; instead of water, we drink soda and alcohol because it makes us feel better. These things has been traditionally passed down from generation to generation. To break this generational curse, we must change how we take care of ourselves. If you want to learn how to take care of yourself better, knowledge is the key; read about it and do your research. There is so much information out there on how to take care of yourself. I was once told it takes 21 days to make a new habit. So, start in small increments; try drinking two glasses of water per day or take a 10-minute walk and build from there. But remember, you must be disciplined and do these things consistently. I know, in time, things will become difficult. This is just the enemy trying to stop you from being better. When this time comes, just call on your Heavenly Father, and these thoughts will flee and set your mind free. In closing, to have a happier and healthier life, you must be willing to change how you think, how you act, and how you talk about yourself.

Lady Shepherd
P.O.G.
Loving Ministry

Body

HEALTH/WELLNESS

HOLISTIC PRACTICE

....

Most allopathic medications either inhibit or eventually altogether prevent the body's ability to function on its own. A drug is taken to suppress symptoms as a solution, for a bodily function, or as a substitute for a bodily substance. As an example of drugs suppressing symptoms, let's look at a migraine: a drug numbs the nerve, thus preventing messages calling out pain from reaching the brain. As an example drugs serving as a substitute for a bodily function, let's look at constipation. An allopathic doctor may prescribe a muscle relaxant, but a holistic practitioner always seeks the cause of the constipation first. The cause may be impacted waste due to improper diet, parasites, candida that clogged the colon, or even inadequate amounts of water which make the stool hard. With all of these causes, sending the muscle the pharmaceutical message to relax won't address the problem and, in fact, may make the constipation worse. Finally, as an example of a bodily product, let's look at the thyroid hormone. If the gland is underactive, thyroxine is prescribed to replace what the gland does not appear to be secreting, but this may cause the thyroid to become more lethargic. Biochemically, the receptors for thyroid hormone are sated. They don't know or care that the hormone they're receiving is from a source outside rather than inside the body; the body's internal sensors know only that there is enough thyroid hormone circulating in the bloodstream for the moment. Our goal is to support the body before it reaches the point where radical intervention is necessary or is the only option; to achieve this goal, we need a holistic approach.

Head Shepherd
P.O.G.
Loving Ministry

HEALTH/WELLNESS

HOME REMEDY ON HOW TO GET RID OF PHLEGM

Good morning, people of God. I hate it when I am out with my friends, and I am having a conversation, and the next thing I know, I have mucus in my throat. It is the most uncomfortable feeling ever. It makes you feel so self conscious. Because as soon as you go spit it out, people are giving you the look like you are so disgusting. Having mucus in your lungs is usually because of the flu or an infection in your upper respiratory system. Even though this is not a serious issue, you have to eject the mucus from your body, or it can cause an irritation of the bronchi and lungs, causing an infection in the upper respiratory system. Here are five home remedies to help get rid of mucus: 1. Honey has anti- fungal properties and helps strengthen the immune system. 2. Lemon water can help eliminate phlegm and mucus from the throat. It is rich in vitamin C and has antibacterial properties, which help the body become resistant to infections. Drink lemon water along with honey and/or hot tea three times per day. 3. Chicken soup warms the airways and soften secretions. 4. Toast can help eliminate phlegm by help carrying it down to the stomach. It scrapes the throat by removing the secretion. 5. Add one gram of echinacea leaves to a tea bbag and prepare echinacea tea by adding the tea bag to a cup of boiling water and letting it brew for five minutes. Drink it twice per day.

Lady Shepherd
P.O.G.
Loving Ministry

Body

HEALTH/WELLNESS

HUNGER

....

1 Samuel 14:33

Then someone said to Saul, "Look, the men are sinning against the Lord by eating meat that has blood in it."

"You have broken faith," he said. "Roll a large stone over here at once."

Good morning, people of God. Have you ever grabbed a handful of chips, eaten a few cookies, or ordered a hamburger through the drive-through, then asked yourself why? The Cornell Food and Brand Lab reported that Americans are eating more frequently due to the availability of fast, convenient food and advertising that creates a temptation to eat even when they aren't hungry. In the study, a total of 45 undergraduate students rated their hunger level before they ate a carbohydrate-heavy meal. The participants' blood glucose levels were then measured at regular intervals after eating the meal to assess how the food impacted their health.

Participants who said they were moderately hungry before eating the meal tended to have a lower blood glucose after they consumed carbs. Although it is easy to grab a quick bite without thinking about it, doing so can lead to spikes in your glucose levels, which can develop into hyperglycemia, prediabetes, or diabetes over time. Whatever you do, please don't go to the other extreme and skip meals, as it can backfire and lead to weight gain and slowed metabolism. So, always check your level of hunger; ask yourself if you are hungry or just bored, tired, stressed or thirsty. Look for physical symptoms of hunger, such as stomach growling, or empty feeling. So, drink water; it is easy to confuse the signal for thirst with hunger. Drink a glass of water before you eat. Don't like water? Spruce it up with lemon, or drink sparkling water. Or keep some healthy snacks with you to increase your vegetable intake by eating some baby carrots, or raw broccoli. It will curb your feeling of needing to eat. Or find a hobby; do something while watching television, like needle work or a jigsaw puzzle – something that will keep your hands busy. Remember, the idle mind is the devil's playground.

Lady Shepherd
P.O.G.
Loving Ministry

Body
HEALTH/WELLNESS
INFLAMMATION

....

Problems are not stop signs, they are guidelines. Inflammation is the body's way of dealing with irritation, whether it is caused by chemicals, friction, heat, pathogens, or toxins. The area becomes inflamed due to two factors: 1. Various types of scavenger cells travel to the site to ingest dead and damaged tissue, acting as a cushion or barrier between the injured tissue and surrounding areas. 2. Increased amounts of blood bring nutrients, oxygen, and hormones to the repair site. Inflammation is different from infection, although one may arise from the other if it persists over time. It can lead to serious diseases like cancer, heart disease, diabetes, arthritis, and Alzheimer's. These diseases occur when the immune system becomes so overactive that it attacks your body's own cells and tissues. While most people are aware that anti-inflammatory drugs can reduce inflammation, few people consider the role of their diet. Pharmaceutical medications and the food we eat are made up of chemicals and compounds, which have biological effects on our bodies. A healthy diet is beneficial not only for reducing the risk of chronic diseases, but also for improving mood and overall quality of life.

Head Shepherd
P.O.G.
Loving Ministry

Body

HEALTH/WELLNESS

KIDNEY STONES

Never give up on a dream just because it takes too long to accomplish it. The time will pass anyway. Kidney stones, also called nephrolithiasis, urolithiasis, or calculi, are small, hard mineral deposits that form inside your kidney. They may affect any part of your urinary tract system. If the kidney stone moves or blocks part of the urinary tract system, it can cause severe pain. Most kidney stones will naturally pass from the body without surgery. But if you feel constant pain, cannot pass urine, or get an infection, you may need to have the kidney stone removed. Sometimes the stone is too big to pass from the body; in that case, you will need surgery to remove it. Staying hydrated can help pass kidney stones faster. Certain substances, including apple cider, vinegar, and lemon juice may help dissolve kidney stones, making them easier to pass. Be sure to drink one eight-ounce glass of water immediately after drinking any flavored remedy. This can help move the ingredients through your system. Apple cider vinegar contains acetic acid. Acetic acid helps dissolve kidney stones. In addition to flushing out the kidney, apple cider vinegar may help ease pain caused by the stones. Other common uses for apple cider vinegar are to lower blood pressure and reduce cholesterol levels. Add one to two tablespoons of vinegar to one glass of water and drink it on an empty stomach immediately before eating. Believe in yourself and unleash the unstoppable force within! You've got the power to achieve well being.

Head Shepherd
P.O.G.
Loving Ministry

Body
HEALTH/WELLNESS
KNEE PAIN

Knee pain is a common complaint that affects people of all ages. It may be the result of an injury, such as a ruptured ligament or torn cartilage, or a medical condition, including arthritis, gout, or an infection. Many types of minor knee pain respond well to self care. Physical therapy and knee braces also can help relieve knee pain. Fruit has received a lot of positive press. Fruit is a highly beneficial nutrient, packed fresh from nature and a portable alternative to candy, cake and other sweets. Although we often combine fruits and vegetables as though the two are in the same category, in truth, they have quite different properties and functions. Fruit contains minerals, vitamins, and fiber. Home remedies can improve your comfort levels and help you manage symptoms. Tai chi is an ancient Chinese form of exercising both the mind and body that improves balance and flexibility. Being overweight or obese can put additional pressure on your knee joints. A heating pad can help relieve pain while resting your knee. Cold treatment can help reduce inflammation. Herbal ointment like cinnamon, ginger mastic, or sesame seed oil are topical pain relief treatments. Believe in the Heavenly Father and know he is capable of healing you of all things when you believe.

Head Shepherd
P.O.G.
Loving Ministry

Body

HEALTH/WELLNESS

LEMON WATER

....

Start drinking a tall glass of lemon water as the first thing you do each morning. The natural concoction is known for its beneficial effects on your overall health, from boosting your digestive system and immunity to encouraging natural cleansing. A simple squeeze of fresh lemon is jam-packed with potassium, vitamin C, vitamin B, calcium, magnesium, antioxidants, and iron. Water is essential for health and energy; however, many people don't appreciate the taste of plain-old H_2O. Try squeezing a small sliver of lemon into your water. In fact, you can slice a few lemon wedges to toss into your water bottle to promote healthy hydration all day long. Drinking a cup of lemon water on an empty stomach before bed will help you lose weight! The citric acid in lemons may help prevent kidney stones. Drinking lemon water provides not only citrate, but also the water you need to help prevent or flush out kidney stones. Adding lemon to your water may help you drink more throughout the day and keep you hydrated. Staying hydrated is critical to good health, so drinking lemon water is pretty much a win-win. Isaiah 58:11 The Lord will guide you always; he will satisfy your needs in a sun-scorched land and will strengthen your frame. You will be like a well-watered garden, like a spring whose water never fails.

Head Shepherd
P.O.G.
Loving Ministry

Body

HEALTH/WELLNESS

LIVING WATER

People who are careful to limit their intake of pharmaceuticals, or who avoid taking them entirely, may still unknowingly ingest all kinds of drugs every time they take a sip of water.

Detectable levels of drugs exist in virtually everybody's water today worldwide. How do drugs get into our water supply? The metabolites are excreted in urine, and hospital personnel flush expired and unused medications down the toilet. Consumers are sometimes advised to do the same, and drug companies do so as well. Drug companies pump waste from the manufacturer of pharmaceuticals into nearby convenient water bodies. These chemicals are not by most municipal filtering systems, which use even more chemicals to treat the water rather than the much safer, and very effective methods, using carbon filtering, violet light, and ozone. Growth and change are painful, but nothing hurts as much as being stuck where you don't belong. You are one decision away from a completely different life. Ordering a glass of water at a restaurant might seem like a boring choice. However, drinking water is very healthy for you. Your body craves water, as it should since it's 60% of your being. It supports every system in your body and does wonders for the condition of your skin and hair. There are so many health benefits of drinking water. If you're interested in drinking better water, inbox me about the Keegan Water Machine. Change your water, change your life.

Head Shepherd
P.O.G.
Loving Ministry

HEALTH/WELLNESS

LIVING WITH DIABETES

Good morning, people of God. I have two kids who have been diagnosed with type 1 diabetes. It is a hard disease to control, but you can live with it as long as you discipline yourself. We had a scare: when my daughter was 14, she decided that she was over it and refused to take her medicine. She ended up in the ICU with a blood sugar level of 371. She went into ketoacidosis, which means she had too much acid in her blood. This can kill you. She started having shortness of breath, vomiting, confusion, dehydration, fatigue, and frequent urination. It is one of the most frightening things you can ever go through. A lot of people told me, "Oh, she is just a teenager, and they do this, because their brains are not fully developed yet. So, they have no rational thinking when it comes to responsibility." That made me feel some type of way. My daughter was diagnosed with type 1 diabetes at the age of two. She has been living with it practically all her life. I am having such a hard time believing what they said about teenagers. So, my solution is to do it the old-school way and start giving her the medication myself. Is it the best solution for an active teenager? No. But our kids needed that hands-on training for life.

Lady Shepherd
P.O.G.
Loving Ministry

Body

HEALTH/WELLNESS

LOSING WEIGHT

....

Everybody wants a great body, but no one wants to work out! Rather than relying on the bathroom scale to tell you if you're overweight, experts say you should also know your body mass index. While your weight may influence how you feel about yourself and even how others view you, body image is not the only reason you should embark on a weight loss journey. In fact, for those who are overweight or obese, losing weight actually carries innumerable benefits beyond looking great in your clothes. When you have strong motivations to lose weight before embarking on your journey, you lose more weight than those who are less motivated. Walking benefits your posture by increasing your awareness of your muscles and overall body and forcing you to think about your form. It also creates stability and eradicates imbalances in the body. One of the best things you can do to become healthier is to base your diet on whole, single-ingredient foods. By doing this, you eliminate the vast majority of added sugar, added fat, and processed foods. Furthermore, eating whole foods also provides your body with the many essential nutrients that it needs to function properly. It's not until you have lost everything that you are free to do anything.

Head Shepherd
P.O.G.
Loving Ministry

Body

HEALTH/WELLNESS

MEDITATION

Some people meditate as part of their spiritual practice; others do it to release stress, relax, and improve their health; still, others do it for mental and emotional clarity. Whatever meditation technique is employed, the goal of all meditation is to increase mindfulness. Mindfulness may be defined as the quality of being attentive, aware, and centered, or grounded, in oneself. With meditation, you can calm the mind down. Instead of being lost in your mental chatter, imagine starting your day with more calmness and clarity. Meditators achieve more vitality and energy, decrease their heart rate and blood pressure, decrease their blood lactate levels, strengthen their immune function, increase their resistance to infection, and significantly reduce their pain levels, including imrpovements in their headaches, migraines, and backaches. Meditation also creates the need for less sleep and improves the quality of your sleep. All you have to do is close your eyes, stay focused on your breathing, and let your mind do its thing. This is one skill where you don't have to strive to achieve something – just a place of stillness where no effort is required. The moment you realize you're lost in thought, return to the object of focus, usually the breath. This is all you have to keep doing – return from your distracted thought to the breath. Envision whatever reality you want for yourself in life. Relax, and let the lord guide you to serenity.

Head Shepherd
P.O.G.
Loving Ministry

Body
HEALTH/WELLNESS
MENOPAUSE

The change of life, or simply the change, is the stage of the human female reproductive cycle when the ovaries stop producing estrogen. This leads to scanty and then a complete end to menstrual periods, at which point a woman can no longer have children. As the body tries to adapt to the changing hormone levels, she may experience heart palpitations and variations in body temperature in the form of day-and-night sweating known as hot flashes. Vaginal dryness and the need to urinate may increase. She may experience depression, anxiety, irritability, and lack of concentration. This process which occurs between the ages of 45 and 55 can last from six months to more than five years. Menopause can be accelerated by serious illness, exposure to poisonous chemicals, autoimmune disorders, thyroid problems, and diabetes. To manage the symptoms of menopause, some women take estrogen replacement hormones; however, unless the estrogen is bioidentical, like what the body itself once produced, this may not help and may even exacerbate her symptoms. Natural progesterone may work better. Caucasian women, particularly of European descent, may have an increased risk of osteoporosis. This can be managed by an increase intake of magnesium, an essential fatty acid, its supplements, or dark leafy greens and fish oils. Menopause is not an illness. It's a natural part of life. Though its symptoms can be difficult to deal with, eating the right diet and exercising regularly may help alleviate or prevent them.

Head Shepherd
P.O.G.
Loving Ministry

Body

HEALTH/WELLNESS

MENTAL HEALTH

The Holy Spirit says to keep guard over your mind, because whatever a person thinks will become their reality. This is why the enemy keeps the world filled with violence, chaos, and murder to keep everyone in fear. Change the way you think to change the way you live and feel. Mental well-being doesn't have one set meaning. We might use it to talk about how we feel, how we're coping with daily life, or what feels possible at the moment. Having good mental well health doesn't mean that you're always happy or that you're unaffected by what you experience. Remember that good days for your well-being won't always look the same; we don't always have the same levels of energy or motivation. Be kind to yourself and do what feels right for you at the moment. Try to think about what might help you to relax. If there's something that helps you, try to find some time to fit it into your day. For example, this could be having a bath or shower, going for a walk, or listening to music. You can also use techniques such as meditation, prayer, or breathing exercises. In addition, spending time in nature can help improve your mood and reduce feelings of stress and anger. Opening up to someone you trust, whether a friend, partner, or family member, can help you feel listened to and supported. Seize the day with confidence. Small steps lead to big achievements. You're capable of overcoming obstacles. Keep your believers alive and let determination guide your journey through life.

Head Shepherd
P.O.G.
Loving Ministry

Body

HEALTH/WELLNESS

MIGRAINE

....

It could be hard to live in this society. This world is forever changing not for the better but for the worse. It could become so overwhelming that it makes your head hurt. Everyone has their opinions, trying to force them to be your beliefs. Headaches occur due to sitting for long periods using your portable device. Your neck muscles become stressed and tight. Circulation decreases by wearing a mask, limiting the amount of oxygen to your brain. You may have a magnesium deficiency. Massage your scalp, and get up and stretch. There are some who have migraines as well, which can be accompanied by distorted vision, nausea, chills, and fatigue. Migraines may be caused by allergies, drugs, chemicals, unsuitable food, a toxic liver, menstrual problems, hormonal conditions, worry, or even strenuous exercise. When you have a migraine, avoid caffeine and other drugs, fake foods, overly fatty foods, and greens. Rest in a dark room. Alkaline mineral water may be helpful, as drinking water has been shown to relieve headache symptoms. Yoga, supplements, essential oils, and dietary modifications are all-natural, safe, and effective ways to reduce headache symptoms. You are a healer with your words. Pray to God to take the pain away. You must believe in order to receive healing. Live your life with a good heart and a happy thoughts. It can keep the pain away.

Head Shepherd
P.O.G.
Loving Ministry

Body

HEALTH/WELLNESS

MODERATION

....

Don't pray for an easy life, pray to be a stronger person. A strong body doesn't become reality through magic. It takes sweat, determination, and hard work. You're there, just keep on going, because your efforts are going to pay off. Hold on, keep your head up, be proud, and do not give up! Accept where you are, and start from there. Once you replace negative thoughts with positive ones, you'll start having positive results. If you do what is easy, your life will be hard. If you do what is hard, your life will be easy. No success comes from laziness; success only comes from relentless effort. Start slowly, and build up gradually. Give yourself plenty of time to warm up and cool down with easy walking or gentle stretching. Then speed up to a pace. You can continue for five to ten minutes without getting overly tired. As your stamina improves, gradually increase the amount of time you exercise. If it's been a while since you last worked out, you'll definitely want to start small. Doing too much too soon can overwhelm you mentally, and a rigorous routine may eventually feel like too much to deal with, which in return makes you feel defeated! Understand that you're probably not going to be as fit as you were, and that's okay. Living in moderation is the key to a successful, healthy, and joyful life. It helps to realize that happiness is not about having more, but appreciating and enjoying what we already have in life. You will be surprised to see that practicing moderation can help minimize stress. Being in mental peace is key to life.

Head Shepherd
P.O.G.
Loving Ministry

Body

HEALTH/WELLNESS

MODERATION 2

Galatians 5:13

You, my brothers and sisters, were called to be free. But do not use your freedom to indulge the flesh; rather, serve one another humbly in love.

Eating food in moderation is key to maintaining a healthy diet. That means you have a little bit of everything rather than gorging on, say, steak or ice cream. "Everything in moderation, nothing in excess." These words have been attributed to many wise individuals over time, including Socrates some 2500 years ago. Moderation is the idea that an individual should avoid extremes, and instead focus on having life commitment, balance, and wholeness. In a society that promotes pleasure-seeking and erroneously equates happiness with having more, the idea of moderation is often ignored. There are many people in this world who are trapped between two worlds: excess and deprivation. However, with moderation, you don't have to put any type of boundaries in your life. The key to a happy, balanced life is moderation. Everything in the world is good when enjoyed in small doses, even if the only apparent benefit is the joy that it brings. So, if you're going to indulge in something, make sure to do it with glee and not guilt.

Head Shepherd
P.O.G.
Loving Ministry

Body

HEALTH/WELLNESS

MORE ENERGY

Colossians 1:29

To this end I strenuously contend with all the energy Christ so powerfully works in me.

Good morning, people of God. We have become a society of easygoing people with no sense of urgency, not trying to perspire or work hard in life. Obesity in America has become a big issue. It seems there is no energy in the people anymore. Hard work has become a thing of the past. No one is willing to go that extra mile. We give up when things become difficult for us. Remember: no pain, no gain. Stop giving up on the one yard line, and go for the touchdown. You must have the strength and vitality required for sustained physical or mental activity. You must fuel your body with the right foods like bananas, apples, eggs, and water. Then, stay in shape; exercise, or take a long walk. Having the right thoughts is great also; see yourself as a lean, mean fighting machine. Be that warrior for Christ; let no enemy stand in your way. Whenever you want to change something in life, it always starts in your mind first. Believe in yourself; have confidence, and have the right attitude. You can achieve all things through Christ. There is nothing you cannot do and nothing you cannot have when you believe in yourself.

Head Shepherd
P.O.G.
Loving Ministry

Body

HEALTH/WELLNESS

MOSQUITO BITES

....

Know your desires; the more you desire, the more you create in the universe. Be accountable and know yourself. Live just to live with a higher awareness of who you are, more importantly, who you are not. Nothing can ruin a fun summer night like a swarm of biting bugs. Bugs like mosquitoes and gnats are known for causing small itchy bumps that take days to heal. These biting bugs usually cause a small localized skin reaction that is a bit of a nuisance but doesn't cause any serious issues. Bug bites can cause swelling, irritation, and itching. Rubbing alcohol may sound harsh, but it is surprisingly effective in treating different conditions of the skin. Rubbing alcohol helps to reduce itching and swelling caused by insect bites, and it can also make your skin less prone to them. Aspirin is most helpful when it comes to pain experienced throughout the body, but it's equally useful for mosquito bites. Due to its powerful anti-inflammatory properties, aspirin can help control the swelling caused by mosquito bites. Grind some aspirin into powder. Then, add a few drops of water to create a paste mixture, apply it directly to the mosquito bite, and leave it on for up to 10 minutes. Wash it off and dry. You should notice the bite getting noticeably smaller, and itchiness should dissipate. You can also cut a lemon in half, and rub the flesh of the lemon over the mosquito bite. Initially, your skin might tingle a bit, but this just means the remedy is working. Rinse the skin with water afterwards to remove any remaining lemon. There are many home remedies; do your own research. Remember: the moment you give up is the moment you let someone else win.

Head Shepherd
P.O.G.
Loving Ministry

HEALTH/WELLNESS

NIGKTCAPS

Ephesians 5:18

Do not get drunk on wine, which leads to debauchery. Instead, be filled with the Spirit.

Good morning, people of God. Have you ever come home from work, relieved that your hard, and stressful day was over, and felt that having a drink will help get you through the rest of the night? Having an after-work beer or an evening glass of wine to help you wind down for a good night's sleep, even occasionally, may not be the best idea. Alcohol consumption, and its effects, can impact your sleep. Researchers concluded that as little as one drink can interrupt the restorative benefits of sleep. Sleeping is a time when your body and brain repair and recharge. For adults, seven to eight hours of sleep are needed to stay alert, process information, and function properly. Alcohol affects automatic bodily functions such as heart rate, digestion, respiratory rate, and other functions during sleep. So, I have some tips for you, P.O.G. family. I know it is unrealistic for everyone to become teetotalers, but I have some other advice for you. Go to bed and wake up at the same time every day. Exercise regularly, and eat a healthy diet. Have a relaxing bedtime routine, and turn off electronic devices. Reduce your fluid intake at bedtime.

Lady Shepherd
P.O.G
Loving Ministry

Body

HEALTH/WELLNESS

NOSEBLEED

A sudden nosebleed can be scary stuff. Most of us have experienced a bit of bloodshed after blowing our nose a little too vigorously; however, frequent nose bleeds can indicate an underlying health condition. Most nose bleeds are a nuisance and stop within five to ten minutes. They usually do not cause enough blood loss to be serious in children or adults who are otherwise healthy. Nosebleeds are common in children because small, delicate blood vessels line the nose and can easily break. What causes nosebleeds? Nose picking, rubbing your nose often, dry air, blowing your nose too hard, having a cold, or allergies. To stop a nosebleed, try to be quiet and calm. Lean your head forward and pinch your nostrils tightly closed. Breathe through your mouth, wet a washcloth or hand towel with cool water, wring it out, and press it firmly to your nose and cheeks. If you seek medical attention for a nosebleed, your doctor will conduct a physical examination to determine a cause. They'll check your nose for signs of foreign objects. They'll also ask questions about your medical history and current medications. Tell your doctor about any other symptoms you've had and any recent injuries. There's no single test to determine the cause of a nosebleed; however, your doctor might use diagnostic tests to find the cause. Chinese philosopher Confucius once said, "The will to win, the desire to succeed, the urge to reach your full potential… these are the keys that will unlock the door to personal excellence."

Head Shepherd
P.O.G.
Loving Ministry

Body

HEALTH/WELLNESS

NUMBER 2

....

Bowel movements are a necessity. They allow you to empty waste from your diet via your intestines. While all people make bowel movements, their frequency varies greatly. You should have anywhere from three bowel movements per day to three per week. Sometimes, the consistency of a person's stool can be a more significant indicator of bowel health than frequency. However, if a person doesn't poop often enough or poops too frequently, it can cause severe health problems. Both soluble and insoluble fiber in the forms of whole grains, vegetables, and fruits can add bulk to your stool, promoting bowel movements. If you don't have a significant amount of these foods in your diet, you may not poop as regularly. Fluids also make stool softer and easier to pass. This is why you should drink more water if you're often constipated. Whether due to illness or changes in activity or diet, everybody experiences a change in their bowel movements from time to time. However, changes that last longer than a week may be a cause for concern.

Head Shepherd
P.O.G.
Loving Ministry

Body
HEALTH/WELLNESS
NUTRITION

You have to feed your mind as well as your body. What you think is what you become. Your mind is a garden: what you plant will grow another aspect of a food. Nutrition is the proportion of proteins, carbohydrates, and fats, or it contributes to the total protein, carbohydrate, and fat content of the entire meal. The nutrient content of a food – the amount of vitamins, minerals, essential fatty assets, enzymes, etc. that it contains – also contributes to one's overall feelings of wellness. People require different amounts of different types of nutrients, depending on their metabolism, level of physical exercise, mental exertion, climate in which they live, and their state of wellness or illness. No one can dispute that good health depends on eating properly. The problem is that even experts in holistic as well as mainstream medical arenas disagree as to what constitutes the optimum diet. There are many types of diets – macrobiotic, vegetarian, vegan, raw food, ayurvedic, complex carbohydrate, low fat, the list is endless. Have you ever asked yourself why popular diets contradict each other so much? How can they be right? You wonder – why does my friend lose weight when she eats certain foods, and I gain weight when I eat these same things, or why does a juice fast make my husband feel great while I just feel tired? Many factors determine the best diet for an individual – genetics, race, cultural practices, body type, season, age, health, environmental toxin exposure, and belief system. These are only some of the many factors to consider in planning an optimal diet.

Head Shepherd
P.O.G.
Loving Ministry

Body

HEALTH/WELLNESS

OBESITY

....

1 Samuel 14:33

Then someone said to Saul, "Look, the men are sinning against the Lord by eating meat that has blood in it."

"You have broken faith," he said. "Roll a large stone over here at once."

Good morning, people of God. I know summer is approaching us slowly, and some of us are trying to exercise to get in shape for the beach body that we so desire. Some of us have given up, because we are too tired to go to the gym or cook and prepare a nutritious meal. It is easier to go to the drive through and get something fast. But, hopefully, after you read some of these figures, it will change your mind. Did you know that more than 35% of adults in the United States are obese? More than 34% are overweight. Did you know that obesity affects 17% of all children and adolescents in the U.S.? Nearly 32% of all children and adolescents are either overweight or obese. P.O.G. family, we are in trouble. Obesity can bring on diabetes, high blood pressure, and heart disease. The only way we can overcome the battle of the bulge is to keep moving. Go for a 30-minute walk, eat more vegetables, and read the labels on the food you purchase, because a lot of what we eat has so much sugar and salt. Drink plenty of water and stay hydrated. I know it's not easy, but something has to be done.

Lady Shepherd
P.O.G.
Loving Ministry

Body

HEALTH/WELLNESS

OSTEOARTHRITIS

....

Osteoarthritis, the most common form of arthritis, affects millions of people worldwide. It occurs when the protective cartilage that cushions the ends of the bones wears down over time. Although osteoarthritis can damage any joint, the disorder most commonly affects joints in your hands, knees, hips, and spine. Osteoarthritis symptoms can usually be managed; although the joint damage can't be reversed, staying active, maintaining a healthy weight, and receiving certain treatments may slow progression of the disease and help improve pain and joint function. Your situation will either be the reason you don't make it, or it will be the story you tell when you do make it. You get to make that choice. Everything you face must also face you. Most people have no idea eating the wrong foods can cause stiff and achy joints. Gluten is found in most foods that are not good for you to eat, such as most bread, pastas, food containing trans fat, alcohol, and sugar. These are some of the worst things you can eat for arthritis. Proteolytic enzymes in food can help treat pain caused by arthritis. Foods that contain these enzymes include berry citrus, leafy greens, broccoli, carrots, bok choy, garlic, turmeric, and ginger. Try adding these ingredients to your food and see how much it will help. If chosen, homeopathic medicines will reduce pain in your joints and improve mobility. Your hardest times often lead to the greatest moments of your life. Keep going through tough situations; they build strong people in the end.

Head Shepherd
P.O.G.
Loving Ministry

HEALTH/WELLNESS

OUR BELLY!

If you'd like, you can lose belly fat without spending a lot of money or needing special equipment. Part of the process is changing what you eat. This does not mean starving yourself or eating grass, but making a few simple changes to your current diet. Adding more movement into your routine and changing some habits are also important. Again, however, you don't have to get radical or work out 80 hours a week. You merely need to make changes in a few of your daily habits. Losing belly fat begins at bedtime. Getting a good night's sleep has positive impact on your ability to lose weight. Your metabolism is hard at work breaking down food into energy while you sleep. It is also regulating various hormones that affect fat cells and how the body uses them. In addition, almost everyone could benefit from a Mediterranean-style diet with its emphasis on fresh produce, whole grains, limited red meat, and healthy fats. Getting off the couch a little more regularly can't hurt either. Anything you can do to reduce your waistline, even if it's a quarter of an inch, can make you healthier. Greatness is built when nobody else is watching. When you focus on problems, you'll have more problems. When you focus on possibilities, you'll have more opportunities. Sometimes, you have to forget what you feel, and remember what you deserve.

Head Shepherd
P.O.G.
Loving Ministry

Body

HEALTH/WELLNESS

OXYGEN

A colorless, odorless, reactive gas, the chemical element of atomic number eight, and the life-supporting component of the air. If you stop breathing, there is no oxygen getting to your brain, and your cells begin to die. Most living things need oxygen to survive! Oxygen helps organisms grow, reproduce, and turn food into energy. Humans get the oxygen they need by breathing through their nose and mouth into their lungs. Oxygen gives us the ability to break down food in order to get the energy we need to survive. Your immune system guards your body against dangerous invaders like viruses and bacteria. Oxygen fuels the cells of the system, keeping it strong and healthy. Breathing oxygen purified through a filter, such as an air sanitizer, makes it easier for your immune system to use the oxygen. Low oxygen levels suppress parts of the immune system, but there's evidence that suggests that low oxygen might also activate other functions, which could be useful when investigating cancer therapies. Take off the mask and breathe like God created you to. The enemy has taken his knee off your neck for the moment, so breathe. You're going to need it, because he's not done yet. You must fight for freedom sometime in life.

Head Shepherd
P.O.G.
Loving Ministry

HEALTH/WELLNESS

PAIN

....

Job 6:10

Then I would still have this consolation–my joy in unrelenting pain–that I had not denied the words of the Holy One.

Good morning, people of God. It's that time of the year again when the seasons change. I remember, when I was younger, my parents used to say, "I can feel it in my bones," and now I am saying it. These millennials don't understand, but one day, they will. Aches and pains in your joints are a form of arthritis. It is from a lack of circulation in your joints and an autoimmune deficiency disorder. A home remedy I recently found out about might help. Boil water with ginger, lemon, or lime and one-third of a clove of garlic, and add honey for taste. Drink this bi-weekly, and you will feel a difference in your joints. Also, medical professionals say you should exercise. They do not mean you have to join a gym. You can walk, ride a bike, or swim – do something to keep moving as long as you are working the joint that you feel pain in. There are some over-the-counter medications that can give you some relief, but you do not want to become dependent on them, because some drugs are not good for your digestive system. If you are a true believer, call on the highest physician which is your Heavenly Father. Ask him, "Father, give me comfort from this pain." Then you must believe without a shadow of a doubt that this will happen for you. This form of medication is called mind over matter.

Head Shepherd
P.O.G.
Loving Ministry

Body
HEALTH/WELLNESS
PARASITE

There are good and bad parasites that live inside of your body. They help your immune system fight off bacteria. Protozoa are some of the bad parasites that come from bad water. That is why it's important to drink clean water. There are others, like worms, bugs, and some insects. We need to do a parasite cleanse twice a year. Make sure the milk you drink and the meat you eat it is not past its shelf life. Cook all meat to its right temperature – above 140 or 160 degrees Fahrenheit. When you are out walking in nature, use bug spray. For intestinal parasites, you can use the following natural remedies: 1. Berberine is a herb that, in several preliminary studies, was found to fight off intestinal parasites. 2. Eat papaya seeds with honey, or honey alone, for seven days. 3. Pumpkin seeds have been found to be high in amino acids, fatty acids, berberine, cucurbitacins, and phenolic compounds. Studies show they help with parasites. 4. Increase your consumption of carrots, sweet potatoes, squash, and garlic. 5. Eat foods rich in vitamin C and vitamin B. 6. Avoid raw meat or fish. If you think you have parasites, it's crucial that you consult your physician. It's very important to take care of your gut, because when it's working right, you feel better about life. Believe your body is working the way God made it to work. You must learn to keep balance in your life by not worrying about every bad thing that happens. Without stress, you will be at your best.

Head Shepherd
P.O.G.
Loving Ministry

Body

HEALTH/WELLNESS

PERIODONTIST

The most common health problem with teeth is the formation of plaque, a soft white layer that contains bacteria, often staphylococcus mutans. The bacteria produce biofilm, which enables them to adhere to the teeth. If the plaque is not removed after a few days, it hardens to become tartar. More serious problems arise when the bacteria produce lactic acid, which dissolves the enamel through demilitarization. However, teeth have been known to renew themselves if the pH in the mouth is at least 5.5. Healthy saliva has an alkaline pH of 7.0 or higher; some practitioners report that if there is an interval of several hours without any intake of food, the saliva can return the dissolved minerals to the enamel and remineralize the teeth. Routine dental visits include a professional cleaning to the teeth to remove plaque and tartar. Regular cleaning and scaling has also been shown to reduce the risk of heart disease or stroke by combating bacteria in the mouth that can infect blood vessels throughout the body. Visiting your dentist every six months may not be the occasion you look forward to most, but it is definitely one of the most important. You should keep regular dental visits, because they do much more than ensuring you have a bright smile. A healthy mouth equals a healthy body. When you smile, the whole world smiles back at you.

Head Shepherd
P.O.G.
Loving Ministry

Body

HEALTH/WELLNESS

PLANTAR FASCIITIS

Plantar fasciitis causes pain in the bottom of the heel. The plantar fascia is a thick, web-like ligament that connects your heel to the front of your foot. It acts as a shock absorber and supports the arch of your foot, helping you walk. Plantar fasciitis is one of the most common orthopedic complaints. Your plantar fascia ligaments experience a lot of wear and tear in your daily life. Too much pressure on your feet can damage or tear the ligaments. The plantar fascia ligaments become inflamed, and the inflammation causes heel pain and stiffness. One of the most common causes of plantar fasciitis is repetitive exertion and overuse of the plantae fascia with inadequately supportive shoes. Plantar fasciitis can also worsen at the end of the day after long periods of standing, or walking. Swelling, inflammation, and stiffness are other symptoms that may be associated with this type of heel pain. However, nearly all cases of plantar fasciitis can be addressed with a pair of over-the-counter plantar fasciitis inserts. Not only do they average around one-tenth of the cost of prescription orthopedic inserts, but they are available in many different shapes and sizes, so you don't have to get rid of the shoes in your closet. To help the pain caused by plantar fasciitis, you can try to fill a shallow pan with water and ice and soak your heel in it for ten to fifteen minutes a few times per day. Be sure to keep your toes out of the water. Teach your body to keep fighting for what's meaningful to you.

Head Shepherd
P.O.G.
Loving Ministry

HEALTH/WELLNESS

PNEUMONIA

Pneumonia is an infection that causes inflammation in the air sacs of your lungs. With pneumonia the air sacs may become clogged with pus or fluid, making it difficult to breathe.

Pneumonia is brought on by either a virus, bacteria, or fungus in the air you breathe. Bacterial pneumonia is more common than viral pneumonia and tends to be more severe. It may develop on its own or occur after a case of the flu or viral cold when your immunity is suppressed. Symptoms include high fever, chills, cough, and sometimes blood in the mucus lining of the lungs. Some home remedies may help a person manage the symptoms and enhance recovery. They include herbs such as peppermint and eucalyptus. Both have a soothing effect on the throat of people with upper respiratory tract infections. These herbs may help break up mucus and ease the pain and inflammation caused by pneumonia.

> James 5:14-16
>
> Is anyone among you sick? Let them call the elders of the church to pray over them and among them with oil in the name of the Lord. And the prayer offered in faith will make the sick person well; the Lord will raise them up. If they have sinned, they will be forgiven. Therefore confess your sins to each other and pray for each other so that you may be healed. The prayer of a righteous person is powerful and effective.

Head Shepherd
P.O.G.
Loving Ministry

HEALTH/WELLNESS
PUSH THROUGH THE PAIN

The mind can achieve whatever you can conceive and believe. Change your mindset, change your life. Embrace growth and surround yourself with positivity. When you invest in yourself, you have the power to improve your life, reach your goals, and achieve greater success. The greatest asset you have is yourself, and the skills, talent, and abilities you possess. It's important to explain and express our emotions rather than suppress them. We might feel like suppressing them will help us avoid pain, but pain is part of life. However, one of the most important things to remember is that pain will pass. Recognize when your emotions are heightened, and take time away from the situation, but instead of suppressing your emotions, shift through them calmly, and eventually come back when you have reached a space where you can address the situation without feeling overwhelmed. Do you ever hear the saying that this, too, shall pass? It will. Getting over and through obstacles in life is normal as long as you learn from it. Nothing is easy in life; take the good with the bad. Keep praying and know that everything is going to be all right. Know that our Heavenly Father loves you.

Head Shepherd
P.O.G.
Loving Ministry

Body

HEALTH/WELLNESS

PUSH YOURSELF

Insanity is doing the same thing over and over again and expecting a different result. In order to take control of your body, you must believe, and be disciplined and consistent with what you do in life. Remember, no pain, no gain. Don't be so quick to give up when things start to hurt. When you push yourself, you get to know yourself. We are only competing against ourselves. It's in pushing yourself that you will come to know your own limits, beliefs, and strengths. The harder you work for something, the better you will feel when you achieve it. You need to do what you don't want to do. If you work hard and keep a positive mindset, your life and body will be shaped for you to achieve greatness. Hard and impossible are two different things. If it was easy, everybody would do it. Stop looking for the easy road, as there is no easy road. Nothing is impossible. The only thing that is impossible is what you make impossible. Just remember, you will never find true success in comfortable situations. Push yourself and your limits. As long as you desire a successful life, you must face your fears and push yourself beyond the limits. Failure to do this will truncate your dream and make your goals unrecognizable. Life does not reward complacency or mediocrity. But, by pushing yourself, you can break through barriers and follow the path that people have not trodden. And, interestingly, once you break through the limit, you will be amazed why you never thought the challenges were surmountable.

Head Shepherd
P.O.G.
Loving Ministry

Body
HEALTH/WELLNESS
REFLEXOLOGY

Reflexology is a type of massage that involves applying different amounts of pressure to the feet, hands, and ears. It's based on a theory that these body parts are connected to certain organs and body systems. People who practice this technique, reflexologists, believe that applying pressure to these parts offers a range of health benefits. Reflexology rests on the ancient Chinese belief in Chi, or vital energy. According to this belief, chi flows through each person. When a person feels stress, their body blocks chi. This can cause an imbalance in the body that leads to illness. Reflexology aims to keep chi flowing through the body, keeping it balanced and disease free. In Chinese medicine, different body parts correspond with different pressure points on the body. Reflexologists use maps of these points in the feet, hands, and ears to determine where they should apply pressure. They believe their touch sends energy flowing through a person's body until it reaches the area in need of healing. A reflexologist's touch may help calm the central nervous system, promoting relaxation and other benefits just like any form of a massage. If you're interested in reflexology, look for a properly trained reflexologist who has registered with the American reflexology certification board. Feel well.

Head Shepherd
P.O.G.
Loving Ministry

Body

HEALTH/WELLNESS

REM SLEEP

REM is an acronym for the rapid eye movement through closed lids that often indicates dreaming. It occurs an average of two hours per night as a normal part of your sleep cycle. A decrease in the amount of REM sleep can be detrimental to psychological and sociological health. When REM sleep is continually interrupted over long periods of time, signs of sleep disturbance occur, including trouble focusing, a lack of motor coordination, and emotional instability. During sleep, our cells are repaired and replaced. Active and stressed parts of the body have time to recharge. The brain removes waste materials from the central nervous system and cycles into different frequency ranges that correspond not only to dreaming and body movement, but also to hormone production, kidney activity, liver detoxification, and more. Regular sleep is crucial to the formation of new brain cells. If you find yourself not able to sleep at night, here are some solutions you can try: Set your thermostat to a cool temperature between 60 to 67 degrees Fahrenheit. Take a warm bath or shower to help speed up the body's temperature changes. Avoid looking at your clock and obsessing about the fact that you can't fall back to sleep. Watch what and when you eat. A meal high in carbohydrates may be detrimental to a good night's rest. Try not to eat less than three hours before you go to bed. Proverbs 3:24 When you lie down, you will not be afraid; when you lie down, your sleep will be sweet.

Head Shepherd
P.O.G.
Loving Ministry

Body
HEALTH/WELLNESS
RNA

....

Speak it into existence! Words are powerful, and we believe our thoughts, so think big and put it into action. Sometimes, believing is the first action. Faith is like when you work out and the muscle starts to grow little by little. Faith is a lot like that, since you believe it before you see it. Call those things that are not as though they were. RNA is a foreign substance that changes our DNA Sequence when it finds a host cell and grows new cells based on that information. This is a brand new platform. There are a lot of people who are skeptical that an RNA vaccine would work. Scientifically, it makes sense, but there's no RNA vaccine out there that has been approved yet. It is not yet known how long the vaccines could offer protection, or whether they would perform well across all age groups or ethnicities. By definition, drugs are supposed to be administered to those who are ill, but there's an entire class of drugs intended to be given only to people who are well-vaccinated. At least, until about the early 2000s, the medical community's official position was that vaccinations should only be given to people presumed to be healthy, because the sick were too immunologically weak to handle the effects that the vaccines were designed to produce. However, the medical community appears to have reversed its original position, and now most doctors routinely advocate vaccinating everyone whether they are healthy or ill. Regardless, good or bad, do your own research on vaccination so you will know the truth. Transformation does not start with someone else changing you; rather, transformation is a reworking of your inner self from what you are now into what you will be.

Head Shepherd
P.O.G.
Loving Ministry

Body

HEALTH/WELLNESS

ROOT CANAL

A root canal treatment is designed to eliminate bacteria from the infected root canal, prevent reinfection of the tooth, and save the natural tooth. Root canal treatment is necessary when the soft tissue inside the root canal becomes inflamed or infected. To protect the tooth, the nerve and the surrounding tooth pulp are removed, and the tooth is sealed shut. The interior of the tooth is left virtually impervious to future decay. The signs indicating the need for a root canal include sensitivity to hot or cold even after the sensation has been removed, swollen or tender gums, a chipped or cracked tooth, pimples on the gum, and severe pain while chewing or biting. An untreated root canal can result in bone loss, infection, and acute abscess, which is a formation of pus on the infected tissue or the area of decay. Some of the symptoms of an acute abscess include unbearable pain, swelling and fever. You can avoid needing a root canal by brushing, flossing, wearing a mouth guard, watching what you drink, and getting regular dental checkups. When you're going through the pain, try to enjoy the process and enjoy the progress. There are times in your life when the most important thing you can possibly be is mentally prepared. This is what makes the difference between those who crack under the pressure of hardships and those who don't.

Head Shepherd
P.O.G.
Loving Ministry

HEALTH/WELLNESS

SADNESS

....

Ecclesiastes 7:3

Frustration is better than laughter, because a sad face is good for the heart.

Good morning, people of God. Do you ever start thinking of situations that make you feel sad? There is so much going on in the world today, so many catastrophic disasters that we have no control over. I know the feeling of sorrow that it is as if no one cares about your emotions. It's hard to get out of bed some days and shake the feeling of loneliness. It is time to call on the greatest physician of all times – your Heavenly Father. Get down on your knees and pray for happiness and brighter days. Do this whenever darkness begins to set in on your heart. You must believe in your words. Faith is believing in the unknown, so keep the faith in knowing your Father hears your prayers. Then, one day, just like a seed that's been planted, your heart will begin to grow with love, compassion, and happiness again. There is power in His name to chase away stormy days, and bring forth sunny days. What you practice is what you will have, so practice being nice to others and loving yourself. Then others will be nice and loving to you.

Lady Shepherd
P.O.G.
Loving Ministry

Body

HEALTH/WELLNESS

SALT BODY

....

It's not hard to eat a lot of salt. Look a little closer at the food you're eating on a regular basis. You might be surprised to find out how much sodium you're actually eating! It has a way of sneaking up on you, because, a lot of the time, it's hidden in our food. The general rule of thumb to follow is anything that is man-made or processed has salt in it, and most of the time it's a lot. While we all need a little bit of salt in our diet to maintain a balanced body, most people get way too much of it, which has damaging repercussions. The human body is a fascinating thing, and because our mind and body are linked, it often has a funny way of telling us when something is wrong when it comes to sodium. Here's a look at some of the strange signs that could indicate you're eating too much salt: You might have noticed that you're really thirsty after eating salty food. That's because salt makes us thirsty. The reason we get thirsty is because our brains react to the amount of sodium that is in our bodies. Eating too much salt can lead to kidney disease or high blood pressure. The solution is very simple: drink more water. This will drive the salt out of your body. A good life is one in which a person develops their own strengths, pursues what they desire, and works toward their full potential.

Head Shepherd
P.O.G.
Loving Ministry

Body

HEALTH/WELLNESS

SEA MOSS

....

P ush yourself, because no one else is going to do it for you; as long as you believe in yourself, anything is possible. Discipline is a foundation to life. The rewards of a disciplined life are great. Sea moss is a sea algae that is commonly found along the Atlantic coast and the Caribbean. It is a sea vegetable that is harvested for its health properties. Sea moss is often described as spiny and red. Although this is true, the color of sea moss depends on where it is harvested from, including the climate and water temperatures that the sea moss is grown in. You might see sea moss that is green, yellow, purple, brown and black. You may know that the body needs about 102 vitamins and minerals for optimum functionality. Sea moss contains a whopping 92 of the required 102 of all of that goodness, making it one wholesome food item. Sea moss vitamins are typically synthetic and effectively absorb into the body. Not only is sea moss rich in vitamins and minerals, but it is also a great source for energy. The two most important days in life are the day you are born, and the day you find out why. Sea moss can be eaten raw or cooked, and it is also available in supplement forms, such as with elin and kye sea moss capsules. Sea moss has many health benefits, including improved cardiovascular health, reduced inflammation, healthier skin, and better digestion. You're never too old to learn and never too young to teach.

Head Shepherd
P.O.G.
Loving Ministry

Body

HEALTH/WELLNESS

SHOWER

Showering cleans the skin and removes dead skin cells to help clear the pores and allow living skin cells to function. It washes away bacteria and other irritants that could cause rashes and other skin problems. From Roman baths to mineral hot springs, cultures around the world have used water for centuries to treat a variety of health concerns. If you have trouble relaxing or falling asleep at night, you might be tempted to take a hot shower to ease the stress of the day. This is a common practice for muscle relaxation before going to sleep, because hot showers activate the parasympathetic nervous system, which makes us tired. Headaches, and migraines, can be blamed on a narrow blood vessel, and can make anyone feel miserable for the most part of the day. However, take a hot shower to stop the pain, because the water reduces the pressure that causes pain. This serves as one of the best remedies that might reduce your need for aspirin. It is also a safe and natural way to handle pain without bothering with medication.

"Everyone who drinks of this water will be thirsty again, but those who drink of the water that I will give them will never be thirsty. The water that I will give will become in them a spring of water gushing up to eternal life," Jesus said.

Do not go where the path may lead, go instead where there is no path, and leave a trail.

Head Shepherd
P.O.G.
Loving Ministry

Body

HEALTH/WELLNESS

SICKLE CELL ANEMIA

Sickle cell anemia, also known as sickle cell disease, is a red blood cell disorder that is passed down from your parents in the same way people inherit the color of their eyes, skin, and hair. There is no way to catch sickle cell anemia, as it is not contagious. Healthy red blood cells are smooth, round, and bendable so that they can easily flow through blood vessels and carry oxygen to every part of the body. Sickle cell disease begins with hemoglobin, the part of the red blood cell that carries oxygen. People with the disorder have a special type of hemoglobin that does not carry oxygen as effectively. After the hemoglobin releases oxygen, it clamps together, forming a stiff rod. This causes the red blood cells to become sickle- or banana-shaped. Sickle-shaped red blood cells are stiff and sticky and don't move freely through blood vessels. This causes them to pile up and block blood flow like a traffic jam, keeping healthy red blood cells from carrying oxygen where it needs to go. This may prevent your organs from getting the oxygen they need. Although these are ways that sickle cell anemia can be harmful to those afflicted, the mutation that causes it actually helps protect against malaria. Therefore, since malaria is common in Africa, both sickle cell disease and several herbs that can help people with the disorder come from Africa. Medical plants you can use include cloves, guinea pepper, grains of paradise, and garlic cloves. What lies behind you and what lies in front of you pales in comparison to what lies inside of you.

Head Shepherd
P.O.G.
Loving Ministry

Body

HEALTH/WELLNESS

SLEEP APNEA

People with sleep apnea stop breathing for 10 to 30 seconds at a time during sleep, up to 400 times every night, waking them for brief periods. This continual sleep deprivation, along with the lack of deep, dream-filled REM sleep, can lead to cardiovascular problems, memory loss, depression, weight gain, and headaches. Conventional doctors often attribute sleep apnea to a failure of the brain to signal the muscles to breathe. The most common allopathic treatment is an electrical device to elevate the tongue, thus keeping the air passage clear. A better, cheaper, and simpler aid that doesn't require a prescription or doctor visit is a rubberized mouth guard that fits over your top and bottom teeth at night. It keeps your airways free and prevents snoring. A good brand you can try is ZQuiet. The cause of sleep apnea is usually snoring or another mechanical issue. The head is pushed unnaturally forward, choking the air supply. If the person is overweight, the soft tissue in the rear of the throat may collapse and block the air passages. In overweight people, it is also important to check their thyroid function. Exercise will help improve respiratory tract efficiency. Specifically, yoga can improve your respiratory strength and encourage oxygen flow by improving your oxygen levels through its various breathing exercises; as a result, yoga reduces the amount of sleep interruptions you may experience. Proverbs 3:24 When you lie down, you will not be afraid; when you lie down, your sleep will be sweet.

Head Shepherd
P.O.G.
Loving Ministry

Body

HEALTH/WELLNESS

SLEEP

....

It's important that you get enough rest each night. Studies have shown you should sleep approximately eight hours each night. In addition, you should not eat less than three hours before going to bed. If possible, limit the amount of meat you eat. It takes longer for your body to digest meat, so if you eat it at night, it will keep you up late. Try not to drink alcohol or coffee before going to bed as well. Also, try not to have electronic devices, like a cell phone, laptop, or television, in the room with you when you go to sleep, because the frequencies will keep you awake. Make sure the room is dark.

If you can, incline the head of your bed at least eight inches above the foot of your bed. It will take some time to get used to this, but, in the end, your body will love you for it.

Meditation can help you sleep also. Some people meditate as part of their spiritual practice. Others do it to release stress, relax, and improve their health. Whatever meditation techniques are used, the goal of all meditation is to increase mindfulness. Another helpful tip is to wake up and go to bed at the same time every night even when you don't have work. This will help your body maintain a regular schedule. When the body is well rested, it is easy to make the right decision.

Head Shepherd
P.O.G.
Loving Ministry

Body

HEALTH/WELLNESS

SLOW DOWN

....

We live our lives in the financial race, trying to beat one another and have the most material possessions, doing the same thing like a hamster on his wheel, day in and day out. When will we stop and take time to smell the roses? Life is a journey, but along the way, you must stop and appreciate what you've already done. There is no doubt that, between work, family, and social obligations, today's modern lifestyle can be stressful. It can be hard to make time for yourself. But it's important to find time to slow down. Relaxing can help keep both your body and mind healthy, allowing you to recover from the everyday stresses that life throws at you. It's simple to learn how to create time for chilling and how to best relax. Just taking a long walk or meditating can help you gather your thoughts. Change the way you eat. Eating more vegetables, fruits, and lean meats can make a difference. Our DNA is from the mother Earth, and you have to consume the things that grow from Earth. What you want to put in the universe is something that has never been done – something unique, something extraordinary, and something that will be remembered long after you're gone. People who make history didn't do it by repeating what others have done. Take one day at a time; don't worry about what's ahead. Live your life in a relaxed state.

Head Shepherd
P.O.G.
Loving Ministry

Body
HEALTH/WELLNESS
SNAKE VENOM

"It is better to fail in originality than to succeed in imitation," said American Renaissance novelist, short story writer, and poet Herman Melville. Symptoms of a snake bite include nausea, vomiting, diarrhea, labored breathing, and fever; in extreme cases, the victim's breathing may stop altogether. The symptoms of a venomous snake bite may look like other health conditions or problems. Antivenom is a treatment specific to the venom of a particular animal or insect. Acorus calamus, Buchanania lanzan stem bark, Moringa oleifera, Achyranthes aspera, and Gynandropsis can all be used as ingredients in antivenom for snake bites. The king cobra is one of the deadliest snakes in the world. The evil one is also a symbol of the snake. He has killed and made people sick all around the world, using its venom to make you sick. God says no weapon formed against you shall ever prosper. You must always have a grateful, thankful spirit.

Head Shepherd
P.O.G.
Loving Ministry

Body

HEALTH/WELLNESS

SORE THROAT

Your throat can be sore for many reasons: microbial infection, food allergies, even pollution. Understanding the cause of your illness may be the first step to easing your pain. Sore throats are among one of the most common health ailments, especially in the winter. Often when your throat is sore, the lymphatic tissue in your neck is swollen as well, and it is said that you have swollen glands. This is somewhat misleading because, in this case, your glands are really lymph nodes, part of the lymphatic system. When the body is fighting an infection, the lymphocytes multiply rapidly, making the lymph nodes swell. Find relief for your sore throat now with these helpful at-home remedies. While salt water may not provide you with immediate relief, it is still an effective remedy for killing bacteria, loosening mucus, and easing pain. Simply mix one-half of a teaspoon of salt into eight ounces of warm water and gargle away. Honey, lemon, hot sauce and herbal teas can help as well. If you have a sore throat, it's recommended that you avoid any foods that may be difficult to swallow. Try sticking to soups and soft foods until pain has resolved. You may encounter many defeats but you must not be defeated.

Head Shepherd
P.O.G.
Loving Ministry

HEALTH/WELLNESS
SPIRIT OF LAZINESS

Proverbs 10:4
Lazy hands make for poverty,
but diligent hands bring wealth.

Good morning, P.O.G. family. Why is it that people want to go through life doing the bare minimum to get by? They never once are willing to go that extra mile. Even at work, you are always doing something, something close to nothing, but different than the day before. We live our lives always trying to live in a relaxed state of mind and body. We come home from work, sit on the couch, and get on social media or watch television until it is time for bed, not willing to improve ourselves by reading a book, going to the gym, or taking a class. In the beginning, this world was built on hard work and determination so you could have it better. People were not afraid of hard work, because they put in a hard day's work for an honest pay. Rome was not built in a day. Why are we so afraid of hard work, wanting everything to be easy? You must put in work to have anything worth having. Your mind tells your body what to do. Make sure you have the right mindset to complete your task. The times of toughness mold and condition you to be who you are. Be strong in the face of the Lord, and let him lead you to greatness.

Head Shepherd
P.O.G.
Loving Ministry

HEALTH/WELLNESS

SPRING CLEANING THE BODY

....

It's springtime, and it's time to do a 21-day cleanse to detox the body again. A full-body detox is a practice that some people believe can eliminate toxins from the body. It may involve following a particular diet, fasting, taking supplements, or using a sauna. Toxins such as poisons, or pollutants, are substances that negatively affect health. The body can already eliminate these substances on its own through the liver, kidneys, digestive system, and skin. Fasting, refraining from eating, is usually done by people for religious, spiritual, or even political reasons. However, some people started to fast for health reasons, originally as a method of cleansing your body. Recently, it has been discovered that fasting, including intermittent fasting, can provide some other important health benefits. A popular form of this type of fasting is called 16 / 8 where, every day, you eat only during a continuous eight-hour period and fast for 16 hours. Intermittent fasting could help you live a longer and healthier life. Ezra 8:21 and 23 There, by the Ahava Canal, I proclaimed a fast, so that we might humble ourselves before our God and ask him for a safe journey for us and our children, with all our possessions…. So we fasted and petitioned our God about this, and he answered our prayer.

Head Shepherd
P.O.G.
Loving Ministry

Body

HEALTH/WELLNESS
STIFFNESS

....

Muscle stiffness occurs when your muscles feel tight, and you find it more difficult to move than usual, especially after a rest. You may also have muscle aches, cramps, and discomfort. This differs from the spasticity of the muscles; your muscles remain stiff even when you are not moving. Muscle stiffness usually goes away on its own, and you can also find relief with regular exercise and strengthening. Sometimes, muscle stiffness can be a sign of something more serious, especially if other symptoms are present. Home remedies are often effective in treating muscle stiffness caused by minor injuries, stress, or overuse. Apply a warm compress or heating pad stretch. Massage, yoga, or tai chi can stimulate your muscles and allow them to relax. Here are some foods to help with body stiffness: Ricotta cheese or cottage cheese are great toast toppers and excellent sources of calcium. Nuts, such as legumes, watermelon, and seeds will work also. However, you will need medical treatment for any serious injury or any underlying health condition that may cause muscle stiffness. The will must be stronger than the skill. Tell your mind what to think. Tell your body how to react.

Head Shepherd
P.O.G.
Loving Ministry

HEALTH/WELLNESS

STINGRAY STINGS

....

It's not about how hard you hit. It's about how hard you can get hit, and still keep fighting. Stingrays are a group of sea rays, which are cartilaginous fish related to sharks. Stingrays are common in coastal, tropical, and subtropical marine waters throughout the world. Most stingray stings are harmless and occur by accident when people come in contact with the spines on a stingray's barbed tail. Some varieties of stingrays are more poisonous than others. Most dangerous injuries require emergency care. To prevent injury, avoid swimming in areas where there are sightings of stingrays. When a spine from a stingray's tail pierces the skin, the sheath around it breaks open and releases the venom, which results in a painful red rash that itches. The sting usually causes a mark, pain, and swelling, which may last several days to several weeks. In more severe cases, life-threatening shock and allergic reactions can also occur. To treat a stingray sting, carefully remove any spines still in the body. Make sure to cover your hand or use a tool to handle the spines. Do not directly touch them or you will be injured. Soak the stings in salt, water, or vinegar. Fresh water will increase pain and may release more of the toxins. Soak stingray stings in hot, but not scalding, water until the pain diminishes. Wash and bandage. If an allergic or life-threatening reaction is observed, go to the doctor right away.

Head Shepherd
P.O.G.
Loving Ministry

Body

HEALTH/WELLNESS

STOMACH PAIN

....

If you want to achieve greatness, stop asking for permission. You must have courage to believe in yourself and all that you are. Stomach pain is something almost everyone is acquainted with at some point in their lives. While some conditions are mild enough to be treated with home remedies, if your pain is severe or constant, it's possible you're dealing with something more serious. So, you definitely want to get to the bottom of that pain. The causes of stomach pain, which can be either acute or chronic, can be related to the appendix, gallbladder, spleen, bowel, liver, genealogical problems, or other complications. A thorough examination and further investigation can help you to understand and properly treat the cause of your pain. While there are many harmless reasons your stomach could be hurting, you definitely want to rule out possible serious conditions. If you're dealing with run-of-the-mill stomach pain, meaning you know exactly what brought it on, like consuming foods that have always been problematic for you or overindulging at a dinner out with friends, you can soothe your tummy troubles with home remedies. For example, the bubbles and the sugar in ginger ale can feed bad bacteria making you sick. You may have heard that lemon water is good for digestion, but keep in mind that acidic foods also tend to be associated with increased acid reflux symptoms. One of the oldest and most popular methods for reducing indigestion and soothing an upset stomach is ginger root. Add it to hot water and sip it slowly. If you think the price of winning is too high, wait till you get the bill from regret.

Head Shepherd
P.O.G.
Loving Ministry

Body

HEALTH/WELLNESS
STOMACH VIRUS

1 Timothy 5:23

Stop drinking only water, and use a little wine because of your stomach and your frequent illnesses.

Good morning, people of God. One strange, long week recently, my daughter along with several other people at work had the stomach virus that has been going around. It turned out to be a very long week – being a short week at work, and coming home and tending to a sick child. The virus has spread all over the Illinois area. If you or your child comes home with cramping, vomiting, diarrhea, and a fever, then it's a clear indication they have a stomach virus. A good habit to get into is to wash your hands frequently. Another thing to do while suffering from this nasty virus is to stay hydrated. Drink sips of water throughout the day. If you can't keep water down, try Gatorade. It will replace your electrolytes. Avoid eating solid foods. It will be too hard to keep down. Try ice chips or chicken broth instead. There is no antibiotic to take for this, so you pretty much have to ride the wave.

Lady Shepherd
P.O.G.
Loving Ministry

Body
HEALTH/WELLNESS
STRESS

....

Romans 13:11-13

And do this understanding the present time: The hour has already come for you to wake up from your slumber, because our salvation is nearer now than when we first believed. The night is nearly over; the day is almost here. So let us put aside the deeds of darkness and put on the armor of light. Let us behave decently, as in the daytime, not in carousing and drunkenness, not in sexual immorality and debauchery, not in dissension and jealousy.

Good morning, people of God. In the news, we have heard about our children being shot down in the streets. People running for political office were accused of rape. Even people we once looked up to as positive role models were accused of rape. Children are disappearing with no way to be found. I don't know about you, but this stresses me out. We have people with power who are making decisions at home that can really damage our lives. I know people say not to listen to the news, but that does not make the situation go away. We need awareness. We need to call on God more often, and pray like we have never prayed before. Things are getting so dangerous out here, and people are suffering around us. I strongly urge you to keep praying for our loved ones. I pray that all who are reading this get some peace of mind. I pray for your protection during your comings and goings. I pray that your children go to school, and return home safely. I pray that you can continue to provide for your family. In Jesus's name, I pray. Amen.

Lady Shepherd
P.O.G
Loving Ministry

Body

HEALTH/WELLNESS

STROKE

The majority of all strokes are ischemic, which means they occur as a result of an obstruction within the blood vessel. This blockage prevents or greatly reduces the delivery of oxygen and essential nutrients to the brain. In some cases, despite testing during a hospital stay, the cause of a stroke cannot be determined. This is what is known as a cryptogenic stroke. It's estimated that 30 to 40% of ischemic strokes are cryptogenic. Atrial fibrillation is a major risk factor for a stroke. It's a common condition in which the upper chambers of the heart beat rapidly and irregularly. As a result, blood is not pumped efficiently to the rest of the body and may pool into a clot. If a clot dislodges, it can travel to the brain and result in a stroke. The best way to prevent strokes is by improving your diet. A low-fat, high-fiber diet is usually recommended, including plenty of fresh fruits, vegetables, and whole grains. If you're thinking of making changes to your diet, you may want to consider cutting or reducing red meat and focus on the use of the 13 plant-based protein sources. Ensuring a balance in your diet is also important. Do not eat too much of any single food, particularly processed foods and foods high in salt. You should eat no more than six grams of salt per day, as too much will increase your blood pressure. Exercise regularly and avoid smoking and drinking too much alcohol. God is saying to you: "I'm giving you grace to deal with the challenges you're facing. Things that used to stress you out will no longer have a hold on you. Let peace guard your heart and your mind."

Head Shepherd
P.O.G.
Loving Ministry

Body

HEALTH/WELLNESS

SALT, SUGAR, AND STRESS

....

From time to time, we have all craved salt or sugar, but if you knew some of the damage they cause when consumed daily, you would think twice about what you put into your body. Although both play an essential role in our health – our brains need sugar for energy and our muscles need salt to contract – when consumed in excess, they can cause a wide variety of health problems. Excess salt intake is associated with increased risk of hypertension, left ventricular hypertrophy, renal stones, and renal failure. Excess sugar intake is directly linked to the risk of obesity, fatty liver disease, and metabolic syndrome. Americans consume about one and a half times the amount of sodium they need and seven times the limit of sugar and added sugar, making sugar the biggest concern. Sugar is linked to a host of other health concerns beyond high blood pressure and heart disease. If you want to flush out salts and sugar from your body naturally, drink plenty of water to flush out all toxins in your body. Consume water-rich foods by eating fruits and vegetables with high water content. Working out and sweating can also help flush toxins out of your system. Stress symptoms may be affecting your health, even though you may not realize it. You may think illness is to blame for your irritating headache, frequent insomnia, or decreased productivity at work, but stress may actually be the cause. Left unchecked, stress can contribute to many health problems, such as high blood pressure, heart disease, obesity, and diabetes. Engaging in activities that support self-care may help reduce stress and anxiety. These can include exercise and mindfulness practices, but in the end, love yourself, love others, and watch what you put into your body. Pray and meditate every day.

Head Shepherd
P.O.G.
Loving Ministry

HEALTH/WELLNESS
SUICIDE

....

Job 40:4

"I am unworthy–how can I reply to you?" I put my hand over my mouth.

Good morning, people of God. In the news, we have seen a lot of celebrities committing suicide. It's odd how we look at them on television and think that they must be really happy, because they can afford a lavish lifestyle, and they're on television smiling. In our eyes, they look like television royalty. We don't realize they are tortured on the inside; it's almost as if they are living a double life. Part of me feels sorry for them, because they are dealing with something that is out of their control, so they seek other methods of medicating themselves. Then some of them just need a little attention, so they attempt just enough to get your attention, which is really scary. I often think that if they don't care enough about themselves, then what will they do to us? God says everyone who calls on the name of the Lord will be saved, and that your body is your temple. God's spirit dwells in you. Knowing that, if I call on the Lord, He will deliver me through whatever I am going through, is such a comfort for me. I realize that you never know what people are going through. That's why you should always treat people with kindness and offer help. Most importantly, pay attention to people's actions, reactions, and patterns of depression. If you are struggling with life or any other situations, there are people who can help you. Call he National Suicide Prevention Lifeline at 1-800-273-8255. You must understand, there is no easy way out of life. You may kill the body, but the spirit lives eternally. So, this "easy way out" is a sin, and your soul will pay for it. When things are getting difficult, kneel, pray, and believe with your heart that your Heavenly Father will hear your prayer. Then, you must start loving yourself again. There is nothing He will not forgive you for. Start loving others, sharing, and caring, and the universe will always give this back to you.

Lady Shepherd
P.O.G.
Loving Ministry

Body

HEALTH/WELLNESS

THE SUN

....

People ignore the benefits of sunshine, even becoming afraid of it during the late 1930s. This was the beginning of the widespread manufacture and use of antibiotics, the pharmaceutical's antibody. Coincidence? Hardly. However, contrary to what sunscreen companies and vampire legends have led you to believe, getting some sun every day is actually quite good for you. The sun loads your body with beneficial vitamins and hormones. You can't see it happening, but you can feel it. It's there when you walk outside on a sunny day and you get that warm hug feeling right before your nice shirt is stained with your sweat. Sunlight helps boost a chemical in your brain called serotonin, the happiest hormone in your brain, which gives you more energy and keeps you calm, positive, and focused. Serotonin also boosts your bone health and might even help treat several skin conditions. Without sun exposure, your serotonin levels dip, which can be associated with a higher risk of major depression and generally feeling down in the dumps. So, before you start journaling about your feelings and getting in front of your television, try getting out in the sun, and see how that makes you feel.

Head Shepherd
P.O.G.
Loving Ministry

Body
HEALTH/WELLNESS
SWIMMING

....

Will you leave fault behind so you can accept responsibility? For the greatest gift one can be given is the chance to begin again. Swimming is not only an intense and effective workout, but it is generally low impact, meaning it won't wear down your joints like running will. Swimming can help you burn calories and fat and improve your heart health without putting too much pressure on the joints in your lower half, such as your ankles, knees, and hips. Swimming has been called the perfect exercise, because it provides all the benefits of an aerobic workout without any damaging impact. It is utilized by athletes to stay strong and fit when recovering from injuries. On top of that, there is no fancy equipment needed – just you and the deep blue. The act of swimming requires the use of practically all of your senses, including sight, sound, touch, and smell. This is a rare opportunity to take a break from your electronic devices. Having water flow over you is relaxing – almost like getting a massage. Swimming is a great way to relieve stress and to become more present in the moment. Don't forget how important it is to love what you do, because if you love what you do, all your efforts, hard work, and sacrifices will pay off.

Head Shepherd
P.O.G.
Loving Ministry

HEALTH/WELLNESS

TAKING CARE OF YOURSELF

You already know that prioritizing self-care is essential for your well-being. Too often, we think of self-care as pampering something that requires a day off and money to disappear to an exotic retreat. But if you think about self-care as less of a luxury, and more as the maintenance needed to sustain yourself, you'll realize how essential it is, and how many opportunities you have to proactively take care of yourself throughout the day and week without retreating to a mountaintop. Maintain a healthy weight and eat a balanced diet that's low in saturated fat and high in fiber found in whole grains to reduce your risk of disease. Specifically, a healthy diet rich in fruits, vegetables, whole grains, and low-fat dairy= can help to reduce your risk of heart disease by maintaining blood pressure, and cholesterol levels. A diet rich in calcium keeps your teeth and bones strong and can help slow bone loss and osteoporosis associated with getting older. Regular physical activity is one of the most important things you can do for your health. Being physically active can improve your brain health, help manage weight, reduce your risk of disease, strengthen your bones and muscles, and improve your ability to do everyday activities. Endorphins are hormones that reduce pain and boost pleasure, creating a general feeling of well-being and positivity. Physical activity increases your heart rate and gets your blood flowing. More oxygen and nutrients to your muscles mean higher energy levels. Never give up. You're amazing, you can do anything, just don't quit, and keep going forward.

Head Shepherd
P.O.G.
Loving Ministry

Body
HEALTH/WELLNESS
TESTOSTERONE

We live in a world of chaos with crazy dictators. The enemy has been planning to destroy mankind for centuries. He feels if he can take away your energy, he can stop you from procreating. In this new age of technology and medicine, he has found new ways to harm us. It is very important that you watch out for toxins in your food and drinks. These toxins will deplete your testosterone in men and estrogen in women. There are chemicals that a plane flies and sprays the clouds with. They call them weather planes, but in actuality you should research chemtrails. There are heavy metals such as aluminum and other toxins in that spray. The spray poisons the soil where our food grows, pollutes the water that we drink, and depletes men's sperm count. The enemy has gotten so crafty that if a man keeps his cell phone in his pocket, it will also deplete his sperm count. This psychotic mad scientist wants to eliminate sexual contact. He has devised a plan, which is synthetic DNA so he can grow the babies in a lab and give them certain traits you can choose from. This is something our Heavenly Father is strongly against. He said to be fruitful and multiply, not to create test tube babies. These liberals and progressives are really getting out of hand. Did you know they are trying to change the law to make pedophilia legal? People of God, it's time to be more aggressive, and stop letting the devil corrupt this world. Stop living in ignorance, and learn about the authorities that you put into office, because the enemy knows that we are arrogant and selfish people and that he can pull the wool over our eyes. We all need to be warriors and speak out against all this injustice in the world. There should not be no one that isn't aware of what's truly going on. AWAKEN!

Head Shepherd
P.O.G.
Loving Ministry

HEALTH/WELLNESS

THIRD EYE

....

Once you can see the world through the all-seeing eye, everything suddenly starts to make sense. Put your heart, mind, and spirit into even your smallest acts. This is the secret of the universe. The chakras are believed to be wheel-like energy centers distributed throughout your body that affect your well-being and perception. The third-eye chakra, also known as Ajna, is considered to be the sixth chakra in the body. This chakra is said to be located in the center of your head, parallel to the middle of your eyebrows. It's believed to be linked to perception, awareness, and spiritual communication. Some say when you open the third-eye chakra, it can provide wisdom and insight, as well as deepen your spiritual connection with God. While the physical eyes perceive the physical world, the third eye sees the true world, a unified whole with an unyielding connection to spirit energy. Don't limit yourself. Many people limit themselves to what they think they can do. You can go as far as your mind lets you. Simply put, the third eye is an energetic center that allows you to tap into your innate intuitive power. With practice, you can learn to work with your third eye through meditation or specific energetic practices by deepening your connection with God.

Head Shepherd
P.O.G.
Loving Ministry

Body
HEALTH/WELLNESS
THERAPIST

....

Now that it is 2021, the world has changed so much. The enemy has caused so much stress, worry, and hatred. People are walking around with short fuses, ready to explode. They don't know who they can confide in or talk to about their situation. Instead, they keep it all inside of themselves to the point of detonation. In 2019, nearly one billion people, including 14% of the world's adolescents, were living with a mental disorder. Do you ever feel too overwhelmed to deal with your problems? If so, you're not alone. According to the National Institute of Mental Health, more than a quarter of American adults experience depression, anxiety, or another mental disorder in any given year. Others need help coping with a serious illness, losing weight, or stopping smoking. Still others struggle to cope with relationship troubles, job loss, the death of a loved one, stress, substance abuse, or other issues. These problems can often become debilitating. A psychotherapist can help you work through such problems. Psychotherapy helps people of all ages live happier, healthier, and more productive lives. It is a collaborative treatment based on the relationship between an individual and a therapist. Through grounding and dialogue, therapy is a supportive environment that allows you to talk openly with someone who's objective, neutral, and nonjudgmental. You and your therapist will work together to identify and change the thought and behavior patterns that are keeping you from feeling your best. To trust God in the light is nothing, but to trust Him in the dark – that is faith.

Head Shepherd
P.O.G.
Loving Ministry

Body

HEALTH/WELLNESS

TIRED

....

Isaiah 40:30

Even youths grow tired and weary, and young men stumble and fall.

Have you ever felt tired and weary of life and felt as if you cannot go on? You wake up in the morning and you just don't want to get up out of bed. You get fatigued just by walking to the bathroom. You sit on the toilet, and you just don't want to get up. You feel that life has beaten you up, and you're ready to give up. I am here to tell you there is something else: there is power in words. Stop believing that you're done. Life has so much more to offer you. Change your thoughts, and change your life. God says, "What a man thinketh is what a man is." Tell yourself, "I am filled with the Holy Spirit. I am all powerful. I will do all things through Christ." Feel the power and tell the enemy, "Lose me and set me free. I am the child of the Almighty." Start taking care of yourself again. Your body is made of 65% water, so stay hydrated, and flush all unwanted toxins out of your body. Eat more fruits and vegetables that give you energy, like pineapples, bananas, apples etc. Stay away from pork and red meats. Eat more chicken and fish. Your body is like an automobile; you have to keep it tuned up by getting exercise. I know some of us cannot join a gym, but there are other ways, like taking a long walk, riding your bike, or simply cleaning your house. If you do some of these things, I promise you, your fatigue will soon fade away, and you will feel more energized. Step back into the ring of life, and this time, you will knock it out.

Head Shepherd
P.O.G.
Loving Ministry

Body
HEALTH/WELLNESS
TUNE-UP

．．．

Your body needs nutrients to tune-up, including vitamins to keep your immune system functioning. It is vital to keep fit in society today. You need to have energy to defeat the dark side. The enemy knows if he can destroy your immune system, he can defeat you as well. Your immune system is your first line of defense to eliminate toxins and viruses from your body. God gave you a belief system so you're able to think for yourself and your wellness. No matter what you are going through, always keep a positive attitude. Your DNA is the same DNA that God has, which contains the power to heal you. Your mind has the capability to heal you. When you're able to connect to the universe and speak to God, there is nothing He will not do for you. Your body needs potassium in alkaline water to help maintain a good immune system. You can put lemon or lime in your water to make it alkaline and eat bananas to help with your potassium. There are also many vitamins that can help boost your immune system, such as zinc, vitamin C, and vitamin D, and there are many foods that contain those nutrients. I know the world has its own medical research, but there comes a time to look into some common cures and find out for yourself what is best for you. Remember to get out, take a walk, and experience nature all around you. During that walk, find a place of peace and meditate about how wonderful life can be.

Head Shepherd
P.O.G.
Loving Ministry

Body

HEALTH/WELLNESS

VIRUSES

....

A virus is a submicroscopic infectious agent that replicates only inside the living cells of an organism. Viruses infect all life forms, from animals and plants to microorganisms, including bacteria and archaea. Vaccines are drugs that actively reduce immune function, because they contain dangerous materials that were never meant to be in our bodies, and thus cannot be metabolized or excreted easily, if at all. The main ingredients in vaccines are pathogens against which we are supposedly being immunized, but there are many other ingredients as well. Some are used as preservatives. Some are irritants intended to stimulate immune cell activity. Other ingredients are supposed to ensure that the pathogens remains inactive – a goal that's almost never accomplished. Any of the substances in vaccines can cause a severe negative reaction. Usually, people aren't told what's in the vaccines if some of the ingredients are common allergens. Not all of these ingredients are found in every vaccine, but most of them are. Since ancient times, herbs have been used as natural treatments for various illnesses, including viral infections. Due to their concentration of potent plant compounds, many herbs help fight viruses and are favored by practitioners of natural medicine. Some herbs that can help you live healthier and that you can try when you cook include rosemary, peppermint, lemon balm, garlic, and basil. Eat well and feel well!

Head Shepherd
P.O.G.
Loving Ministry

Body
HEALTH/WELLNESS
WALKING

It's free. It's easy to do and easy on your joints. It also lowers your risk of blood clots. In addition to being an easy aerobic exercise, walking is good for you in many other ways. Walking wards off heart disease, brings up your heart rate, lowers blood pressure, and strengthens your heart. Walking releases endorphins into your body, one of the emotional benefits of exercise. Depending on the person's weight, a brisk 30-minute walk can burn around 200 calories. Over time, calories burned can lead to pounds dropped. In addition, walking tones your legs, abdominal muscles, and even arm muscles if you pump them as you walk. Furthermore, according to a University of California, San Francisco, study, women ages 65 and older who walked two-and-a-half miles per day had a 17% decline in memory as opposed to a 25% decline in women who walked less than half a mile per week. Walking is a great way to improve or maintain your overall health. Just 30 minutes every day can increase cardiovascular fitness and endurance. Physical activity does not have to be vigorous or done for long periods in order to improve your health. You can make walking an enjoyable, social part of your lifestyle. As your fitness improves, you will be able to walk longer distances and use more energy. Give yourself time to think about life. Be one with nature and enjoy the world around you. Spend time with your Christ conscience and let go of your worries.

Head Shepherd
P.O.G.
Loving Ministry

Body

HEALTH/WELLNESS

WATER

Water is much more than something we gulp to wet our throats. Like the oxygen we breathe, water is essential to life. Our bodies contain an amazingly high amount of water. According to the *Nutrition Almanac*, in a normally hydrated adult, the blood contains 83% water, the kidneys 82%, the muscles 75%, the brain 74%, the liver 69%, and the bones a surprisingly high 22%. All of our vital functions require water. Dr. Susan Kleiner, professor at University of Washington, explains in her article, "Water: An Essential But Overlooked Nutrient," that fluids fill virtually every space within and between cells. Water molecules not only fill space, but they also help form the the structures of macromolecules such as protein and glycogen. As the primary fluid in the body, water serves as a solvent for minerals, vitamins, amino acids, glucose, and many other nutrients. Water also plays a key role in the digestion, absorption, transportation, and use of nutrients. Water is the median for the safe elimination of toxins and waste products. Whole body thermoregulation is critically dependent on it. From energy production to joint lubrication and reproduction, there is no process in the body that does not depend on water. Jesus said to them, "I am the bread of life. Whoever comes to me shall not hunger. Whoever believes in me shall never thirst."

Head Shepherd
P.O.G.
Loving Ministry

Body

HEALTH/WELLNESS

WHY IS ALUMINUM IN PRODUCTS?

....

Remember, you can do anything that you set your mind to, but it takes action, perseverance, and facing your fears. There are two kinds of minerals that humans cannot utilize. The first are commonly called heavy metals or toxic metals. Heavy metals are not nutrients. Poisonous to your body, they should never be ingested regardless of their form. For the purpose of this discussion, aluminum, cadmium, lead, and mercury are commonly regarded as heavy metals. Much of our drinking water contains heavy metals. These heavy metals accumulate in your body, clogging whatever tissues they settle in, eventually reaching your joints, blood vessels, organs, glands, and bones. Once the heavy metals are trapped in your tissues, they interfere with your body's ability to function, causing serious damage. Some of the damage occurs in the form of degenerative conditions such as heart disease, arthritis, respiratory conditions, and dementia. Two of the most common heavy metals are aluminum and mercury. Although aluminum is the world's most abundant metal, it is not needed by the human body to function. To remove heavy metals from your body, try adding blueberries, lemons, or Chaga mushrooms to your diet. Only those who dare to fail greatly can ever achieve greatly. Blessed are they who hunger and thirst after righteousness, for they shall be flled.

Head Shepherd
P.O.G.
Loving Ministry

Body

HEALTH/WELLNESS

WORK IT OUT

Exercise is defned as any movement that makes your muscles work and requires your body to burn calories. Adults who sit less and do any amount of moderate to vigorous physical activity gain several health benefts, both physical and mental. Being physically active improves your brain health, helps manage your weight, reduces the risk of disease, strengthens your bones and muscles, and improves your ability to do everyday activities. Exercise has also been shown to help boost energy levels and enhance your mood. It may even help you live longer. There are many types of physical activity, including swimming, running, jogging, walking, and dancing, to name a few. The secret to experiencing moments of happiness and fulfillment in life is freedom, and the price of freedom is having the courage to act in moments of crisis. The courage to speak the truth in the face of injustice, and the courage to stand up for the noble values that serve you and the ones around you. When the pressure of your times challenge everything you stand for, will you be able to stand uo and fght for what is right, or will you crumble in a corner crippled by fears and doubts? Your choice may have an impact not only on you! The longer we dwell on our misfortunes, the greater the power to harm us is.

Head Shepherd
P.O.G.
Loving Ministry

Body
HEALTH/WELLNESS
WORKOUT

....

1 Timothy 4:8

For physical training is some value, but godliness has value for all things, holding promise for both the present life and the life to come.

Good morning, people of God. Have you ever gone to the gym and stuck to one thing? You wanted to try something else but you were intimidated by the machines and bored with the same old routine? Well, the best way to get out of a fitness slump is to switch it up. If you hit a plateau or would just like to ramp up your fitness routine, try working out with a friend, or joining a fitness class like Zumba or yoga. Whether you are running, swimming, biking, dancing or taking a cardio class, try to incorporate high intensity intervals while working out so that you can burn more calories, build your endurance, and become stronger and faster. When you're on the treadmill, increase the incline, and move those arms. Let's not forget the music. Listening to music while working out can improve your performance. Just remember not to overdo it; take a rest day so that your body can repair your muscles so you can be ready for your next workout. The standard recommendation is to work out for 30 minutes five days a week. Have fun and stay in good health.

Lady Shepherd
P.O.G
Loving Ministry

Body

HEALTH/WELLNESS
WORK THROUGH IT

Happiness is not dependent on what's going on around you. It's dependent on what's going on in you. Hard times, whatever the term means to you, are a common part of life. Developing coping skills can help you get through them more easily. Maybe you're experiencing a financial setback, or someone you love might be facing a health challenge. Maybe you've lost your job, or an unhealthy relationship is weighing you down. You might not be in complete control of these difficulties, but you have a choice about how they impact the way you feel. Reframing your perspective and seeing things from a new angle can help you step away from a negative mindset. Faith without work is dead. So, you must continue to work harder to ensure you manifest your dreams. All your dreams can come true if you have the courage to pursue them. Your intelligence may be confused, but your emotions will never lie to you! Pain is impossible to ignore; as soon as we feel something that hurts, we're wired to start thinking about it to prevent future injuries. Sometimes discomfort is indeed a sign you need to back off. However, most of the time, with proper form and the appropriate exertion or exercise, pain is really just a sign of conditioning or muscle breaking down and building back. Stronger discomfort can signal time to slow down, time to panic, or time to push on even harder, and what your body is trying to communicate is almost entirely dependent on what you want to hear. In any kind of athletic performance, it's inevitable you're going to face discomfort, physical or emotional, but it's your perception of and reaction to it that will determine how much power it has over your performance. No pain, no gain, just push through it.

Head Shepherd
P.O.G.
Loving Ministry

Body

HEALTH/WELLNESS

YOU NEED REST

....

Go to sleep and wake up at the same time as the birds. You will reap the day's golden grains. Eat more green, and you will have legs and a resistant heart like the beginnings of the forest. Look at the sky as often as possible, and your thoughts will become light and clear. Be quiet a lot and speak little, and silence will come into your heart, and your spirit will be calm and full of peace. Good sleep improves your brain performance, mood, and health. Not getting enough quality sleep regularly raises the risk of many diseases and disorders, ranging from heart disease and stroke to obesity and dementia. There's more to good sleep than just the hour spent in bed. With the stress of the COVID-19 pandemic weighing on people over the past years, it's more important than ever to advocate for mental health resources and daily routines that promote physical, mental, and emotional well-being. Rest is vital for better mental health, increased concentration and memory, a healthier immune system, reduced stress, improved mood, and even a better metabolism. Psalms chapter 91 versus 1-2 Whoever the Wells in the shelter of the most high will rest in the shadow of the Almighty. I will say of the Lord he is my refuge and my fortress, my God, and whom I trust. I am a child of the most high God. He chose me, he made me so unique he has made me so creative to change the world! Get rest so you're ready to fight the darkness of this world.

Head Shepherd
P.O.G.
Loving Ministry

Body

HEALTH/WELLNESS

ZINC

....

Vitamins and minerals are considered essential nutrients, because, acting in concert, they perform hundreds of roles in the body. They help shore up bones, heal wounds, and boost your immune system. They also convert food into energy and repair cellular damage. Nearly 100 different enzymes in the body depend on zinc, a mineral involved in skin repair and making DNA, the blueprint for cellular replication. In addition, zinc supports normal growth and development during gestation, childhood, and adolescence. You also need zinc for a proper sense of taste and smell. Furthermore, zinc provides structure by helping to support proteins such as those found in muscle tissue and cell membranes. Zinc is also involved in supporting eye health. Zinc is found in many foods, such as meat, fish, poultry, cereal, and dairy. The amount of zinc that your body can absorb is affected by how much protein is in your diet. So vegetarians, vegans, or people on long-term restrictive diets are more likely to experience zinc deficiency. When you are exhausted and want to give up, that's exactly the moment you shouldn't give up.

Head Shepherd
P.O.G.
Loving Ministry

www.ingramcontent.com/pod-product-compliance
Lightning Source LLC
LaVergne TN
LVHW041709060526
838201LV00043B/640